'Ali boma ye!'

Fans chant 'Ali kill him' at title fight in Zaire 1974

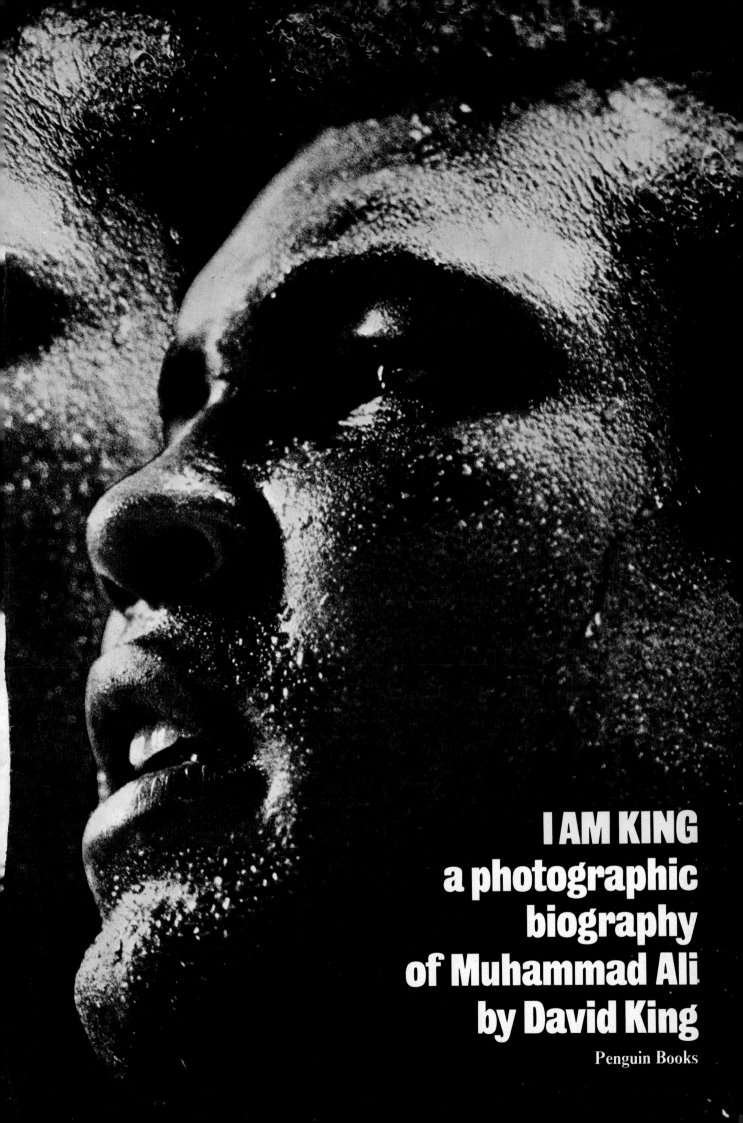

**I AM KING
a photographic
biography
of Muhammad Ali
by David King**

Penguin Books

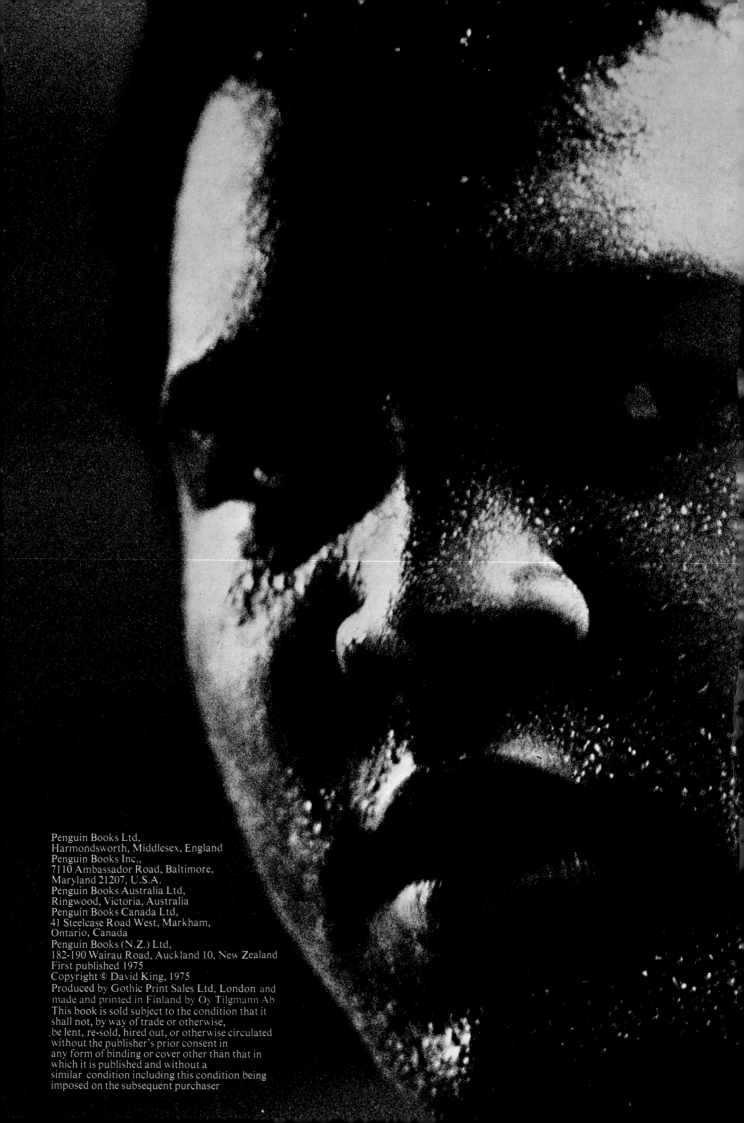

Penguin Books Ltd,
Harmondsworth, Middlesex, England
Penguin Books Inc.,
7110 Ambassador Road, Baltimore,
Maryland 21207, U.S.A.
Penguin Books Australia Ltd,
Ringwood, Victoria, Australia
Penguin Books Canada Ltd,
41 Steelcase Road West, Markham,
Ontario, Canada
Penguin Books (N.Z.) Ltd,
182-190 Wairau Road, Auckland 10, New Zealand
First published 1975
Copyright © David King, 1975
Produced by Gothic Print Sales Ltd, London and
made and printed in Finland by Oy Tilgmann Ab

'The Heavyweight Champion of the whole Plannet Earth'
with his second wife, Belinda, and their four children.
Left to right: Muhammad Iben, two, twins Rasheda and Jemilah, three,
and Maryum, six, at their mountain retreat in Pennsylvania

Odetta Lee Grady Clay, Ali's mother, with her husband, Cassius Marcellus Clay Sr, in the sitting room of their Kentucky home

'My son is everybody's champion'

Mr and Mrs Clay and Muhammad's younger brother, Rahaman Ali, recall their memories of the champion. Opposite page: Cassius Marcellus Clay Jr, 12 years old

Mrs Clay I remember when he was five or six years old. He always liked to play with older children. He told them what to do and wanted to be their daddy. From the age of 12 he trained every day. He never took part in anything else since he stepped into the gym. Fred Stoner worked the children too hard. He kept them up too late. He used to train them at night because I think he had another job during the day. I took them away because of that. They were too late getting to bed.

One day he left the new bike we had bought him outside the Columbia Gym. It was stolen and he went into the gym in tears and told Joe Martin who was a patrolman as well as a boxing instructor. Joe Martin asked him if he wanted to learn to box. My son said he did, so that he could beat up the person who stole his bike if he ever found him. So the next evening he went along there and he really liked it. He's never looked back. When he was 12 he said he'd bring back the Olympic Gold Medal and that he'd be champion of the whole world. I believed him. It's really been a sacrifice for him, it wasn't easy, he trained so hard.

Rahaman This is true of all great scholars, all great men. My brother was born through my mother and father by God to be World Champion. To be known by the people. To liberate the people.

Mr Clay He was born to be a leader.

Rahaman He was born to be a mission. He's supernatural almost. He's a beautiful person. He's not colour conscious. His intelligence is superior to any other fighter.

Mr Clay I was the right father for him. Not stupid like most fathers.

Mrs Clay He was not the top student at school. He wasn't interested in anything else besides boxing. He was just a fair student. He didn't participate in other sports.

Mr Clay Louisville's rich and I don't mean money. I mean rich in nature, rich in colour. It's got plenty of green. I see this, I'm an artist. I still paint signs from time to time and I do oil painting. My son has still got a chance to go to art school. It takes a lot of money to be an artist and he has that now.

Rahaman We had one hour a day for gym. That's all he did, other than box. He was very fit.

Mrs Clay I always believe that he will win. But now I am older I can't take it. It gets on my nerves. I've been to almost all his fights. I feel he can take care of himself, but I can't take it anymore. I went to Zaire. I couldn't miss that. It was all so wonderful.

Boxing was dying before he came along. They all say that he revived it.

Rahaman My brother says boxing did die after Joe Louis. The Italians had a great champion in Rocky Marciano. Each race has their own champion. If people aren't interested in boxing it's because there is no white hope. People want a champ who looks like them. Everyone wants the success of their people.

Mr Clay My son is everybody's champion.

Rahaman My brother was just born to box.

Mrs Clay When he was 18 months old he punched me right in the mouth. It loosened one of my teeth. I didn't go to the dentist. By the time I did it had affected all my front teeth. Now I have a bridge. I can't smile too much now. They've never been the same since. Belinda is a nice sweet person. I couldn't have a nicer daughter-in-law.

Rahaman She's been a Muslim all her life. She's had a completely kosher diet. She went to an Islamic school. Her whole life is based on the Islamic way. She says if Muhammad went another way than Muslim, she would leave him. She's very dedicated, she has to have a Muslim husband.

When you go back to England, be sure to tell them how well you were treated, how you were given real Kentucky hospitality. We are very warm people, Sir, we mean it from the bottom of our hearts.

Rahaman He turned professional in 1960. He got a sixth-round decision in Louisville against someone called Hunsaker in his first fight. Our father negotiated the contract with Bill Faversham. Our father wanted to put my brother in the best hands. He pushed some people aside. Fred Stoner was in his corner for his first professional fight, then the syndicate of 11 Louisville businessmen contacted Angelo, who has trained him ever since. Chris Dundee is the brains of the Dundee family. The oldest in relation to boxing. He taught everything to Angelo. He's the undercover man, he calls his shots from under the table. My brother is in the best hands he could ever be in. When he first began boxing The Louisville Sponsoring Group did a good job for him. But Herbert

Top left: The original Cassius Marcellus Clay, the abolitionist. It is believed that Ali's father was named after him in gratitude for freedom from slavery. Left: Cassius is greeted by his mother, father and brother at Louisville Airport on his victorious return from the Rome Olympics. Above: The home in which the Clay brothers were raised, 3302 Grand Avenue, Louisville. Right: The brothers help their great-grandmother on her way to her 99th birthday party in July 1963

Muhammad has done a better job for him. Understand he doesn't do anything without consulting his father, the Honourable Elijah Muhammad. We love people; we know the value of people. I know this: I'm closest to my brother. I know his disposition.

My brother, he introduced me to Islam. He had become interested in 1960 at the beginning of his pro-

fessional career. He brought it to me in 1961. I accepted it three months later. I've not looked back since. We have temples all over America. It was in Temple 29 in Miami that the minister taught my brother Islam. It has changed us mentally, physically and morally. It has made us more intelligent, cleaner – I mean hygiene – we understand the nature of people more. There is a golden rule – respect everybody but don't turn the other cheek. If a man hits you, hit him back. But never be the aggressor. No Muslim should go to war. Everyone has their own mind; we are all independent. Every Muslim – we all say – our life is more rewarding than as a Christian. Cassius Clay was limited. Muhammad Ali is unlimited. The word is universal. Islam is universal. The belief is the same –

God is Allah. Muhammad is his messenger. The problems of the black people in America are different from our brothers in the Arab countries. We have to liberate our people from the mental slave teachers. We can have freedom once we believe it. We are not Negroes, we come from Africa. 'Negro' was a word used to identify us from our brothers all over the world. We were robbed of knowledge of our homeland. Allah came to America and talked to Elijah Muhammad for $3\frac{1}{2}$ years about how to liberate us. I think the reason the Establishment didn't like us, can be explained by this parable.

If I come in to your room and you are asleep and I start taking everything and you wake up and start screaming and I say, 'Shut up and go back to sleep.'

Now I've got everything and you saw me take it. They enslaved us and the Indians. We helped to build this country, now they don't want any trouble. We say, 'Give us something.' The writing's on the wall. Why don't they give us something? If a man works for me, I pay him. We worked for 400 years – they don't repay us. The Establishment is afraid now. They know we want repayment.

I enjoy talking the truth. We are peaceful people. We don't carry weapons. Allah is with us. We have his protection. I used to think we were all in the same society. It isn't true. Animals don't try to integrate. Bluebirds fly with bluebirds, don't they?

Every name we are given has a meaning. Ali means

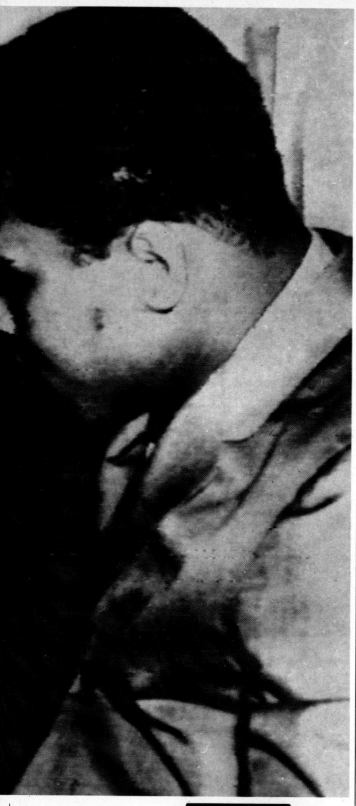

Above left: Rahaman, Elijah Muhammad Poole, leader of the Black Muslims, and the new World Champion of 1964.
Left: Ali with Malcolm X in Harlem, 1964. Top: Wedding day with Belinda, 18 August 1967. Above: Raymond Boyd, Belinda's father, holds up photos of his daughter and son-in-law in his home at Blue Island, Ill. He is a member of the karate-trained section of the Black Muslims, Fruit of Islam

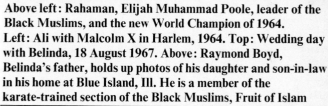

'the most high'. Muhammad means 'praiseworthy'. Rahaman means 'beneficent' – to have much love, to love much. I'm trying to live up to my name. I love people, Sir. Mr Muhammad saw this in me.

My name was Rudolph Valentino Clay. I dropped the last name because it's a slave name. Every black man has a slave name, an English name. I'm from Africa; I'm not English. When we accept Islam we are freed from

Above: left to right, Mr Clay Sr, Lentoi Roi, Mrs Clay and
Sonji Roi, Ali's first wife, at ringside for the second Liston fight.
They were married in 1964, but Ali complained she could
not live up to the demands of the Islamic faith and they were
divorced early in 1966. Below: Ali's first visit to Africa
in June 1966. Opposite page: The return to Africa in 1974 with
Rahaman for the celebrated
'Rumble in the Jungle'

slave-masters' names.

'X' means I am no longer 'Clay'. 'X' means I'm
waiting on a name from God. Mr Elijah Muhammad is a
prophet. He has the right to name us all. He will free
Black America. He is divine. Malcolm X was no influence
at all on my brother. Mr Muhammad taught Malcolm X.
He was one of Mr Muhammad's ministers. But he
became jealous, he thought he could outspeak him, told
lies about Mr Muhammad. He turned against Mr
Muhammad. People didn't like him telling lies. He died
for that – telling lies on a good man.

My brother and I ran a little gang when we were
kids, six or seven guys. There was another gang further
up the city. We had gang fights, but we never fought
much between ourselves. We've always been close. He
lives near me in Chicago. I'm glad he does. He bought a
marvellous mansion – three storeys, 16 rooms.

The happiest moment of my life was when my
brother won the championship. I can honestly say more
than when I first saw my newborn child through the
screen. Ever since we were little boys he said he'd be
world champ. The night he did it – it went through my
mind – a whole lifetime. When he raised his hands,
I cried like a baby.

He always said to my mother that if he was successful
in boxing he could buy her a new home and a Cadillac
and make sure she had a lot of money in the bank. He has
done just that. My brother's life has been like a fairy tale,
Sir, especially for me.

Joseph Elsby Martin, with patrolman's son, relaxes in his Louisville home

'I started that kid out'

Joseph Elsby Martin (above, with Cassius after he had won the 1959 National Golden Gloves Trophy) is a patrolman with the Louisville police force. He trained Ali during his amateur days and now heads the Amateur Boxing Programme in Louisville. Opposite page: the Olympic Light Heavyweight Gold medallist takes the stand

The gun is a .38. I had it chromium-plated. A patrolman is always on duty. I never take it off. I've been with the Louisville Police Department for 34 years. I don't want promotion. I've got too many outside interests. I don't have room for police work all the time.

Fighters now aren't as tough as they used to be. They don't get the exercise. They used to have to work railroads and things to develop their muscles and their hands. Now if a youngster is in a corner fight, his mother calls up the police, the sheriff, the hospital. In my day, if I got my teeth bust in, my Dad wouldn't even look up from his newspaper. He would have said, 'You better learn to fight or get off the street.' People don't have the discipline over their youngsters any more. Clay was OK with me because I'm a police officer and a strict disciplinarian. I never had any trouble with him. He was a perfect gentleman, never made any remarks about girls or anything like that.

Once we took a plane to California for a fight. It was a bad flight and Cassius was scared to death of planes anyway. So on the way back, I said, 'Here's your plane ticket, or you can walk. I'm going by plane.' He walked, hitched-hiked all the way back to Louisville.

We first met at the Columbia Gym. He was 12. He had come to get goodies from the black merchants' market, balloons and things. He had his bike pinched and he came to see me to report it because I was a police officer. He said he was going to whip the guy who took it. I said he better learn to fight first, if he wanted to whip him. Clay was religious about learning – he trained

Cassius's Golden Gloves years. Above: Quiet exit after kayoing Tony Madigan for the Inter-City Light Heavyweight title. Opposite: Training in 1959 with Johnny Hampton. Inset: Defeating Gary Jawish in the 1960 heavyweight contests, New York City

every day.

I trained him for six years. One time I disciplined him for something and stopped him coming to the gym for a bit. So he went to Fred Stoner for a while.

After Cassius won the Olympic Medal, we had a contract drawn up between Bill Reynolds (a prominent Louisville businessman), myself and the boy. We were going to give his father $20,000 for signing it. Then Clay's lawyer, Alberta Jones, came in and said Mr Clay wouldn't sign a piece of paper with my name on it. Billy Reynolds wouldn't sign it alone because he was already a multimillionaire and he needed a fighter on his books like a hole in the head.

I don't remember Mr Clay turning up at any of his son's amateur fights. I would have remembered if the old man had come down to the gym, sure to God, but I don't remember. The mother, she turned up a few times. He never turned up.

I had a lot of fun with Cassius, I enjoyed it. I used to have a TV show in Louisville called 'Tomorrow's Champions'. I predicted when he was 15 that he'd do this well. Everyone thought I was nuts. Clay was a kid that not too many people liked. They didn't like his talking. He's hated here in Louisville.

Clay's biggest mistake was joining the Muslims.

They wouldn't let him go in the Army. He would have been a big man in the Army. People disliked him because of his mouth; it wasn't a race thing too much. My mother always taught me that all children were God's children. This determines your attitude when you're older. He wasn't interested in the Muslims when I first knew him. Malcolm X was a big influence on him, no question about it. I don't think he'll leave the Muslims, there's no way out. I know some of his Muslim friends personally. I can't say anything much about them. They've always been very courteous to me.

I head the Amateur Boxing Programme in Louisville, but I don't see any more Cassius Clays coming up. His secret was speed and coordination. Ted Williams, the baseball player, is the only athlete I can compare with him. I don't know about Pele, I've never heard of him. Clay was completely unique. I showed him how to develop his speed and coordination. He's not a strong puncher because of his speed. Punching is like lifting a weight – you need your feet planted firmly on the ground. A punch comes from the legs. I showed him how to cut. I teach all my boys how to snap.

He was a cocky kid, but he worked hard at it, he trained hard. I started that kid out. Whoever teaches you that system, that style, it stays with you the rest of

your life. I've never met a man who didn't think he could whip someone. Cassius thought he could whip them all! Boxing goes way back. It's still in man's system. They like to feel masculine. It's a great sport. I've taken a lot of kids, delinquents, into my gym. Boxing throws the spotlight on them. They don't get into much trouble after that. Most kids that come into boxing are very aggressive.

I bet on Clay for the first Liston fight. I was sure that Clay could beat him. Liston was not too sharp. Say 'Hallo' to him and he'd be stumped for an answer. Cassius was always devoted to boxing, never had any girl friends that I knew of. I don't think he needs to retire soon. This thing about punch-drunk fighters – mostly they were born punch-drunk – not too much brains to start with.

I've been auctioneering for about 12 years. It's good fun, interesting. I hold auctions all over the country. I'm financially well off, I don't owe nobody nothing. Like Mr Reynolds, we could have made a lot of money out of managing Cassius, but we didn't need to. And you wonder, with all these tragedies that have happened with people connected with him. His lawyer, Alberta Jones, she was murdered down there by the river. Then the deaths of some members of The Louisville Sponsoring Group and Malcolm X too. No one's ever investigated.

I always carry a gun. As a patrolman you always carry a gun. I came home one night and caught two fellas emptying out my house. When they saw me they ran. I shot them right there on the steps. One of them was in hospital for six months. Another night I caught a fella trying to break out of my house. I said 'Stop!' but he didn't, so I shot him. I don't aim for the legs like some police do. I shoot so they won't get up, that's what a gun is for. A couple of guys tried to hold me up in the street. They had a jump-knife. I held my gun right between their eyes. I said, 'You're lucky, you've run into the biggest comedian in the police force.' I sent them to the penitentiary for two years. I could have blown their brains out.

Above: The 1960 U.S. Olympic Boxing team, with Cassius arrowed. Welterweight Willie McClure (fourth from left) and middleweight Sergeant Eddie Crook (far right) were also Gold medallists. Right: The new Olympic Light Heavyweight Champion enjoys his international fame

I know a lot of people in this town. I was asked to run for sheriff, but I wasn't interested. I'm doing too many other things. You need a lot of money to go into politics in this country. The mayor of this city spent $300,000 on his campaign. He only gets paid $25,000 a year for his four-year term. So he's down $200,000. But he doesn't mind because he's a multimillionaire. It's just a pastime. I know these people.

There's too much welfare in this country, anyone can get it. If I asked for it they'd give it to me and I've got a nice house in Louisville, three cars and a holiday home in Florida.

It's been a year since I've seen Cassius. We get on well. There's no animosity. I still call him Cassius. He don't say nothing about it to me, he's no dummy.

The Olympic Light Heavyweight Final. *Boxing Illustrated* reported: 'Zbiegniew (Ziggy) Pietrzykowski was a southpaw. He had tormented and ripped up all his opponents in the prelims and semi-finals. Now it was Cass's turn. Only by tearing the Pole apart, bloodying him and nearly knocking him out did Clay get the unanimous decision.' It was the culmination of 106 amateur fights. According to Martin, 'I trained Cassius for all his amateur fights. He lost eight. One of those was against Jimmy Ellis, I shouldn't have let Clay go in, he was sick, but he insisted. Another he lost on a split decision in the 1959 Pan American Games

against a southpaw named Amos Johnson. Cassius always had trouble with southpaws. One time when Cassius was sixteen I threw in the towel. He was fighting someone called Green who was much older. The year before doctors had found Cassius had a heart murmur. Although it went away, I didn't want to see him get hurt. He was getting beaten all right and I knew Green would knock him out if it wasn't stopped. Cassius said he could've gone on, but I hate to see my boys hurt.' Apart from these few setbacks, Clay had had a brilliant amateur career and when he came home he was flooded with offers to turn professional

Fred Stoner, right, one-time trainer of Muhammad Ali,
with his latest prospect, Kevin Wooden, in the Grace Community Centre gym, Louisville.
Stoner says Wooden, 15, will be as good as Ali in three years' time

'The black boys are the best'

Fred Stoner was one of Muhammad Ali's early trainers. He took an interest in Ali as an amateur and was in his corner for his first professional fight. Opposite page: Ali's brother, Rahaman, helps strengthen his stomach muscles in 1960

I've been a trainer at the Grace Community Centre here in Louisville for 27 years. I work from nine in the morning till 11 at night, Saturdays too. You get used to it. This would be a terrible place if we didn't have the Centre. There's a great need for it. When school's out, the kids are all over the place. Even the little ones are smoking marihuana and popping pills. They start off on diet pills and they get up there on cloud 14. They'll take anything. Cassius and his brother were brought up carefully, didn't even smoke. Their mother kept a tight rein on them.

Cassius used to go down to the Columbia Gym. He fought a young guy called Jimmy Davis, who beat Clay. When his parents saw the calibre of boys we had fighting and realized that their sons had to compete with them, they asked me if Cassius and his brother could come up here to train. Mr and Mrs Clay came along for about three months to watch them, then they let them come alone on their bikes.

Clay was serious, he was a good boy. Rudy would have been capable had they kept him going. In a lot of respects he was a better fighter than his brother. He could have beaten Cassius but he idolized him and put all his interest into the idea that his brother was on top. Cassius got on fine with his parents, no problems.

Natural ability in boxing? There's no such thing. It's like picking a diamond out of the ground. It has to be polished up. Has to be developed. There's no such thing as a born fighter. I suppose Cassius was a hungry fighter – he didn't come out of an affluent family. He didn't have it too easy! We are all out of the same bag. It's an ordeal.

Kids here are competitive from the beginning. Little children even are thrown right into this conflict. I see them outside. You gotta run or fight. If you run, you're his meat from then on. You take a beating every time you turn round if you can't fight.

Cassius liked sports with single opponents – man-to-man combat. He wasn't interested in basketball, or any team sport like that.

His talking shouldn't be taken too seriously. It was all gingerbread and cheesecake for publicity. He got the idea from a wrestler called Gorgeous George who was always bragging in the same way. If he hadn't talked so much he would have been like any other guy. It kept him in the limelight.

When people go to see a fight they like to see a blood bath. We haven't come that far from the Roman arena. The public wants to see blood and guts. I'd like to see it on a more technical level with no knockouts. Most people think heavyweights should just stand and bust each other's brains out. It doesn't make sense to me. If you're going to be a couple of toe-to-toe sluggers, why go through all this training? I prefer the British style of boxing, to learn to defend yourself, man to man. It's more scientific. You try to analyse the way a boxer thinks. I noticed in Clay's boxing that he didn't like to be hit. That's right, why should he stand and be banged like a drum? His head's not a drum and his body's not a gong. This is a smart fighter, it's the guy who uses his brains who lasts. Some boxers are like shooting stars – they go up and come right down again.

The average kid today wants to be a star from the start. They don't want to do the training, it takes sacrifice. Clay had determination and willingness to learn the skills of boxing. Constant practice over and over the things you have to do.

Cassius was always thoughtful of other people. I remember when he found out Step'n Fetchit, the old comedian, was down here in a charity ward. Clay took him out and put him on his feet again.

Angelo was good for him. He had the connections. I can just teach them what I know, but you need money to move them. The black boys are the best. I tried to get some teachers here to form a cooperative. They were too short-sighted and wouldn't do it. Then they blamed me for turning the boys over to the white people.

For his first three pro fights he came back here to train. Then he joined The Louisville Sponsoring Group. I think it was the right move. Without them he wouldn't have made it to the championship. He wasn't misused. Because of the trust fund they set up for him, he'll never be broke like so many other fighters.

As for the Army test, they said he was stupid – I'd like to be that stupid! They deprived him of his livelihood, took his title. They took away his visa so he couldn't fight in other countries. It was a miscarriage of justice. How could they have done that? Just because of a boy's sincere belief. He was no draft-dodger. He wouldn't budge, I glory in his spunk. He could have made millions. They robbed the public of seeing him at his peak.

This must be a real bad country with the cops going round with .38s, black jacks, Mace and things. And still we've got the highest crime rate in the world. It's hardly safe to walk the streets at all.

'He never wanted to hurt a guy... unless, of course, they made him mad'

Bill Faversham, right, represented the group of eleven wealthy businessmen, calling themselves The Louisville Sponsoring Group, who managed Ali's professional fights for five years until the Muslims took over in October 1966

I first became interested in boxing at the age of 10. My father used to take me to the old Madison Square Garden to see the fights. I boxed at prep school and Harvard and I've never lost my interest in it.

I first saw young Clay boxing in the Golden Gloves, and when he started winning in the Olympic try-outs I became very impressed. I was having a dinner party and Pat Calhoun and I were playing bridge in the TV room, when word came over that Clay had won the try-outs. Pat and I said to each other, if that boy wins the Olympics we might do something about it. He won, and when he got back he was flooded with offers.

I arranged to meet Cassius and his family. They all came to my home with Alberta Jones, who was a good lawyer. We discussed the whole proposition. They listened intently. I said I didn't want someone making a few bucks out of him and letting him go. I told them that we would take him along slowly. Money was no object. Cassius and Alberta Jones understood what I was saying. A lot of guys don't look after their fighters. We formed a syndicate of 11 businessmen. They were all millionaires except for me. The family signed us because we were the right type of people.

We sent Cass over to Archie Moore for training, but after three weeks Archie said, 'I can't do much with him, he's so strong headed. You're wasting your money.' I said he needed a good spanking and had him shipped back. So we did a deal with Angelo Dundee who knew Clay through his fights in Louisville and thought he was a great kid.

Angie is a smart little cookie. He's the best man we could have got. No one has that much effect on Cassius except Cassius. Once Angie was talking to a reporter at the gym. He said, 'You're going to see a new blow that Cassius is developing,' and demonstrated it. Cass overheard him as Angie intended, and went in to spar using it and used it in his next fight. If Angie had said it to him straight, Cass never would have used it. This way it was his own invention.

Once Cass sparred with Willie Pastrano, one of Angie's fighters. He made Willie look so silly after one round that Angie wouldn't let them in the ring together any more.

Cassius's one idea was to become Heavyweight Champion younger than Patterson. We didn't believe he was ready in 1963 to meet Liston. He argued and said that if we didn't get him the fight he'd get it himself. So I called up Eileen Eaton, a promoter friend of mine who knew a Catholic priest with a lot of influence over Liston, to let Liston know we didn't want the fight that year. It had to seem as though the idea came from Sonny and sure enough he agreed. Maybe it was for tax reasons.

So he fought Cooper in England. That was an historical fight because somebody had the poor taste to buy Clay a crown which he wore into the ring. In that fight Clay played around. I went to the corner and he said he wanted the ref to stop the fight because of Cooper's eye. Cass had a funny streak in him. He never wanted to hurt a guy. He didn't like that, unless of course they made him mad.

Clay signs professional contract with The Louisville Sponsoring Group, 25 October 1960. Left to right standing: Mr Clay Sr, Bill Faversham Jr, W. L. Lyons Brown Sr, James Ross Todd and George W. Norton, IV. Seated: Pat Calhoun Jr, Cassius and Vertner D. Smith Sr

In February 1964 we signed him up to fight Liston. No one would bet on Clay, there were no takers. Before the fight, he had been seeing a lot of Malcolm X. Angie and I became suspicious. We knew Rudy had already become a Muslim.

At the weigh-in with Liston, Cass started behaving like a deranged man, trying to fight Liston. It took three of us to hold him. There was talk of the fight being called off because of Clay's hysteria, so we sent Dr Pacheco round later in the afternoon to give him a check-up. Cass was lying on the floor of his room watching TV with some neighbourhood kids. According to Pacheco he was the calmest guy in the city, so the fight went on.

Cass did a beautiful job on Liston. He was the first guy who was bigger than Liston. Sonny would stare down at his opponents to terrify them during the opening ceremonies, but he couldn't do it against Cassius, he had to stare up. Sonny was the kind of fighter who didn't mind dishing out punishment but couldn't take it himself. He got worn out by round seven and didn't get up.

We didn't have a party after the fight, because Cass announced that he'd joined the Muslims and we considered it too dangerous because feelings were running very high. His mother was a bit upset at the time but it didn't stop her loving him, and she soon got used to it. I've never met his Muslim wife, but I did meet his first wife and she was a heck of a nice girl. She wouldn't wear the long robes that Muslim women wear, she wore short skirts. She was always very protective of Cassius.

That was the first year the syndicate made any money. Cass was always in debt to us. One time before a major fight he said to me, 'I want that Cadillac I seen. You guys got enough money. You buy that for me.' I said OK because I didn't want him going into the fight in a bad state of mind. We wrote it off as a bad debt.

Mr Clay Sr was a bit difficult at times. He didn't want us to invest his son's money for him. He said, 'What do we need you fellas for – investments, securities? I know all about it, I just never had the money to do it.' He said that to us and we had some of the best business brains in the country in our group.

If he'd only kept his mouth shut about the Army for one more hour, he wouldn't have been taken in his second test. I found that out in a peculiar way that I can't divulge. They only wanted skilled labour at that time. They didn't want the trouble of training him for anything. But he sounded off at a press conference that he wouldn't do his service before I could get word to him.

His exile caught him at his peak. Clay in his prime could have beaten Joe Louis and Marciano, but he never fought in his prime. The Group stopped managing him when he decided that he wanted to stick with his own men, the Muslims. A lot of the Group were losing interest by that time anyway. We were getting old. Cass couldn't have been more gracious. He told us six months in advance and thanked us publicly in the ring. It all ended on a very pleasant note.

I'm very fond of him still, but I don't go to any fights now because of my heart.

'We got a big slug of money and the championship'

Gordon Davidson, above, was the attorney for The Group

We prefer not to use the word 'fixing'. We negotiated the contracts and handled the business end of things. We paid Clay around $1,500 for his first pro fight. Boxers aren't worth much when they're starting. We paid all expenses and gave him 50 per cent of the gross. Later we changed it to 60–40 in his favour. There was no way that he could lose money, but we were in the red until the third year. We wanted to see a local boy do well and be successful. Initially we were more interested in that than making bucks.

I thought Liston was sure to win in the first fight, I bet on him. I negotiated it as if it was his last fight – the end of the road. My sentiments were, 'Let's get as much out of it as we can.' I was the most surprised guy in the world when he won so easily. We got the best of both worlds – a big slug of money and the championship.

Clay's relationship with his family was very close. Maybe his father liked to assert himself, but really we had no trouble with the family. There was a fine parental relationship; Ali showed great deference to both of them. He was very close to his brother: they were always together. We had his brother on the payroll. We put him on preliminary bouts.

Muhammad should be making big money now, no trouble with taxes, and we set up a trust fund for him. He gets it at 35 or when he retires, whichever comes first.

The relationship between Muhammad and the Group was rocky and emotional at times, but it started and ended on a good note. Of course, the Muslims were always there in their black suits glaring at us, but they didn't cause any problems.

'There's some kinda nut downstairs, wants to talk with us'

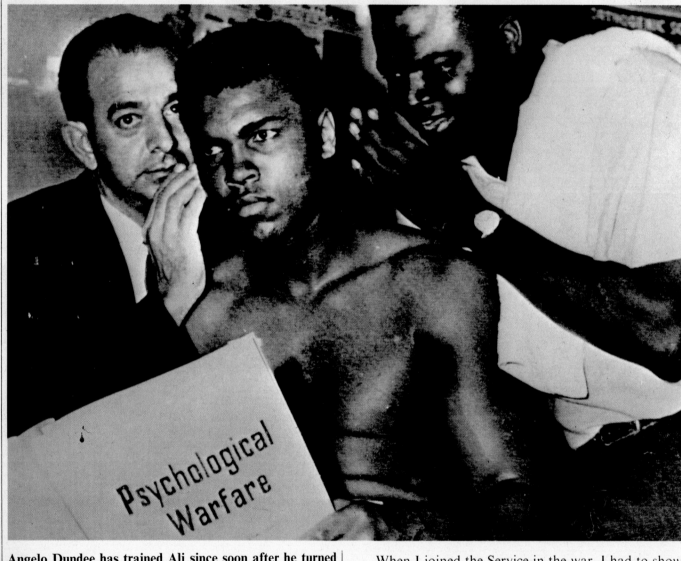

Angelo Dundee has trained Ali since soon after he turned professional. Above: Angelo, Ali and Bundini Brown prepare battle plans for the first Liston fight, February 1964

OK, let's bat the breeze!

My dad was a track layer on Hog Island with the railroad. He only made 24 bucks a week and there were seven of us to support.

He was the governor of our house in those days. It was an Italian family! He used to lick my brother and me when we made too much noise sparring together in his bedroom. It was South Philadelphia, a rough neighbourhood. I was so short and dumpy, they used to call me Porkie. You had to learn to take care of yourself there. I was in about three street fights a week.

That's where I got *my* training.

When I joined the Service in the war, I had to show them I could look after myself. I took on the toughest fighter in the unit. A big guy, but I had the fight brains and he was just a slugger, so I beat him easy. Nobody bothered me after that.

One day a guy saw me hitting the heavy bag. He said, 'Why don't you fight for us.' I didn't know it at the time but he was just looking for cannon fodder. But when you fight in the Service they give you steaks and things instead of cheese sandwiches and the kind of food they usually dish out. So I said OK. I had 12 fights at welterweight, and I won them all. Twelve for twelve. I even fought coming over on the boat to England in 1943. We were stationed at Newbury. It was fine, but when those buzz bombs came over . . . You see they were

meant for London, but sometimes they overshot and then, WHAM! Those guys, those Germans! Really crazy.

Until the war, I'd never gone anywhere, or seen anything. I could have stayed on Stateside, but if you were walking around Stateside in those days you felt like a slacker. I remember being on trolley cars and old ladies looking me up and down seeing if I'd got a broken leg or arm or something. People would say, 'Why aren't you over there, when my son's just been killed?' I was very conscious of all this, that's why I went overseas. I got training in the Service. I got a good education there. I was an aircraft inspector and worked on guidance systems. But it became monotonous and after the war I chucked it in.

I phoned my brother Chris back in New York who was a successful manager. I asked him if I should continue fighting. He said, 'Oh no!' But he had 25 fighters on his books and needed help around the place. I did anything. Typing, shining shoes, wrapping hands, all the odd jobs. But there I rubbed shoulders with the greatest guys in boxing. I used to listen to my brother in the office.

All the big names were there, all the best writers, managers and fighters. I sucked up all this knowledge from them. Then I worked as second man in the corner. I used to go to the fights every night at the Garden which was right across the street. If Helen [his wife] wanted a date with me, she'd have to go to a fight. Afterwards we used to go eat a pastrami sandwich at the Stage or somewhere like that, and I'd take her home to Jackson Heights on the subway. On the way back I'd be so tired I'd fall asleep and end up in Brooklyn.

Then my brother went to Miami, and I stayed behind. But the club dried up. TV saw to that. So I joined my brother in Miami Beach and opened the Fifth Street Gym in 1952. We've been there ever since.

Miami Beach was very lucky for me. I was able to get fighters and develop them. I used to travel to Cuba to work with fighters every week. I even learnt Spanish. I soon got a dozen Cuban fighters on my payroll. Luis Rodrigues, José Napoles, Doug Valliant and others. All became champions or near champions.

Then Carmen Basilio was to fight in Miami and needed a corner man. His manager was sick so I stepped in. It was supposed to be an easy fight, but it turned difficult. It was a tough one and I dealt with all his cuts. It was lucky for me. I got known.

But my big break came in 1959 when I went to Louisville with Willie Pastrano. I was staying in a hotel and got a call from the lobby. This guy says, 'My name is Cassius Marcellus Clay, Junior. I have won six Golden Gloves tournaments in Kentucky. I have fought in the Tournament of Champions in Chicago. I won the National Amateur Athletic Union Championship in Toledo and I am the 1959 National Golden Gloves Light Heavyweight Champion. And I'm going to win the Gold Medal in the 1960 Rome Olympics.' He said he wanted to talk to us.

I said to Willie, 'There's some kinda nut downstairs,

Left: One of Angelo's greatest moments. Hysteria fills the ring after Cassius defeats Liston to become Heavyweight Champion

TUES. NOV. 28 8:30

TOMMY
HICKS

GEN. ADM. '3ᵒᵒ

Angelo's brother, Chris Dundee,
with young fighter at the
legendary Fifth Street Gym,
Miami Beach, Florida.
Ali did much of his
early professional training there

wants to talk with us.'

Willie said 'There's nothing good on TV so send him up.'

He came in with his brother Rudy who was carrying a plaster sculpture of Cassius under his arm and a painting he'd done of him. Rudy, Muhammad and the father are all very talented artists. Cassius announced that he was going to win the Olympics. That was one year before he did.

After that I saw him from time to time, I used to be in Louisville quite frequently. It was a good fight town in those days. After the Olympics, Cassius said, 'How come you never make any approach to manage me. Why don't you want to manage me?'

I said, 'If you want to, you can come down and train at the gym anytime.'

He replied, 'You don't understand, people have been offering me thousands of dollars, Cadillacs and things.'

The Louisville Sponsoring Group signed him up and sent him over to Archie Moore in the salt mines. He didn't get on there. He wanted to be the star and there were two stars. Over there Archie was the star. So Faversham gave me *carte blanche* with him. He'd heard about me through the TV fight shows I arranged. I said to Faversham to send him down after the Christmas holidays. But the kid wouldn't wait. He said, 'Every day is Christmas, but I wanna fight now.'

So he arrived in Miami by train and I put him in a hotel in the ghetto area. In those days, it was 1960 and the South, they wouldn't allow coloureds on the Beach, not in the restaurants, nowhere. The kid didn't mind, he liked it. He was full of pep and ginger.

He was the first in the gym and the last out. I took him up gradually. He had got a lot of good amateur fight education, but the transition to professional is a big jump as anyone in the business will tell you.

All fighters are different and you have to treat them different. With Muhammad I had to let him think he was the innovator. I used to say, 'That's a good left uppercut Muhammad. I love the way you bend your knee when you bring your fist up. Perfect.' Or, 'That's a great belly jab,' and then he starts throwing great belly jabs.

He used to do those shuffles in his amateur days, I've seen film of it. The shuffle confuses his opponents, makes them mad, and it's flash!

Muhammad used to look frail at the beginning, before he got big. He never lifted no weights. You know, people don't realize his career was in jeopardy early on because of his hands. He had protruding knuckles, which is also the reason that his punches hurt so much. A lot of doctors looked at them and wanted to operate. But I said no. I don't believe in interfering with a man's tools, something could go wrong.

The poetry is not good poetry, is it? Just good for a boxer! I'm a bit of a poet myself. I started the name picking. The Bear, the Rabbit, the Mummy. I know the value of publicity. He's the most available superstar in the world. He changed the old thing about 'My manager does de talkin', I do de fightin'.' He'll talk to anyone, from schoolgirls to priests. He doesn't smoke, doesn't

Louis Seria has worked in Ali's corner since Angelo brought him over from Cuba in 1960. Rahaman says of him, 'Seria is the best masseur in boxing. He tells him, or he used to, how much training to do. But now no one tells my brother what to do'

drink. He does other things alright, but they don't affect your health!

I learned something early on. Never mess with a fighter's personal life or religion. I've never had any problems with the Muslims. When Herbert Muhammad took over it was OK. He trusted me.

Ali trained for four months for the Foreman fight. It was the longest he'd ever trained. Foreman got in better shape after his eye cut, but the long wait in Zaire got him down. My guy had the experience to take it.

Muhammad's had problems before, like in Lewiston, Maine, when six guys in a tomato-red Cadillac threatened to kill him before the Liston fight.

With the Foreman fight we were ready for any tactics. One fight has nothing to do with another fight. You can't plan anything 'cos when the bell goes it's him out there, not me. But it goes so fast you don't have time to worry. I knew Muhammad would win.

The staying on the ropes wasn't planned. Foreman formulated his own defeat. Muhammad's a professional. He made the guy useless. He licked him with his strong points, so what was the guy going to do with his weak points? Muhammad was his most difficult opponent. He stood 6ft 3ins to him, eye to eye. But Foreman's not finished, he just talks and acts that way. You've been kingpin of the world, and then a guy negates you. It's a lousy feeling.

Slacken the ropes? Why would I do that? I check the ropes every time I go out of town. Except here in England that is. Here the guys know what they're doing.

No, they got it all wrong, thought I'd out-smarted them. I tightened the ropes, well, you turn them a little, the wrong way, you know. They thought I'd loosened them. What would be the point? Now, if I tighten them, he can bounce right off them.

Muhammad will stay in boxing as long as he's on top, as long as he's winning. My guy likes to fight. He loves it.

Bundini Brown and his wife Cora May

'Ali wins because that's what God made him for'

Bundini Brown, right, is Ali's spirit-builder and constant companion. Above: Ali, Angelo, Rahaman and Bundini play about in the gym while in training before the Liston fight

I've been with Ali from the beginning. We won the championship together.

I'm his spirit. God speaks through me. I'm Hebrew, not Muslim, but it's the same God, and Ali believes that. Angelo couldn't do my job and I couldn't do his, but I can add a lot to it.

This planet is for the people – you and me and her and her. You shoot the jelly in the belly and out comes life. God is my daddy, and I love him. He knows that. That's why he treats me good. But he's a jealous daddy. If you don't love him he won't treat you as good as he treats me.

Now I *know* that and I didn't get no schooling. Think of the word 'woman'. It's got both words there. I think God could have been a woman. You're my son, you've only been on this planet 6,000 years. Man started in Africa, all life comes from there.

These were the boots Ali wore for the first Frazier fight. They are size 13 – you need a solid foundation for all that frame. Ali wins because that's what God made him for.

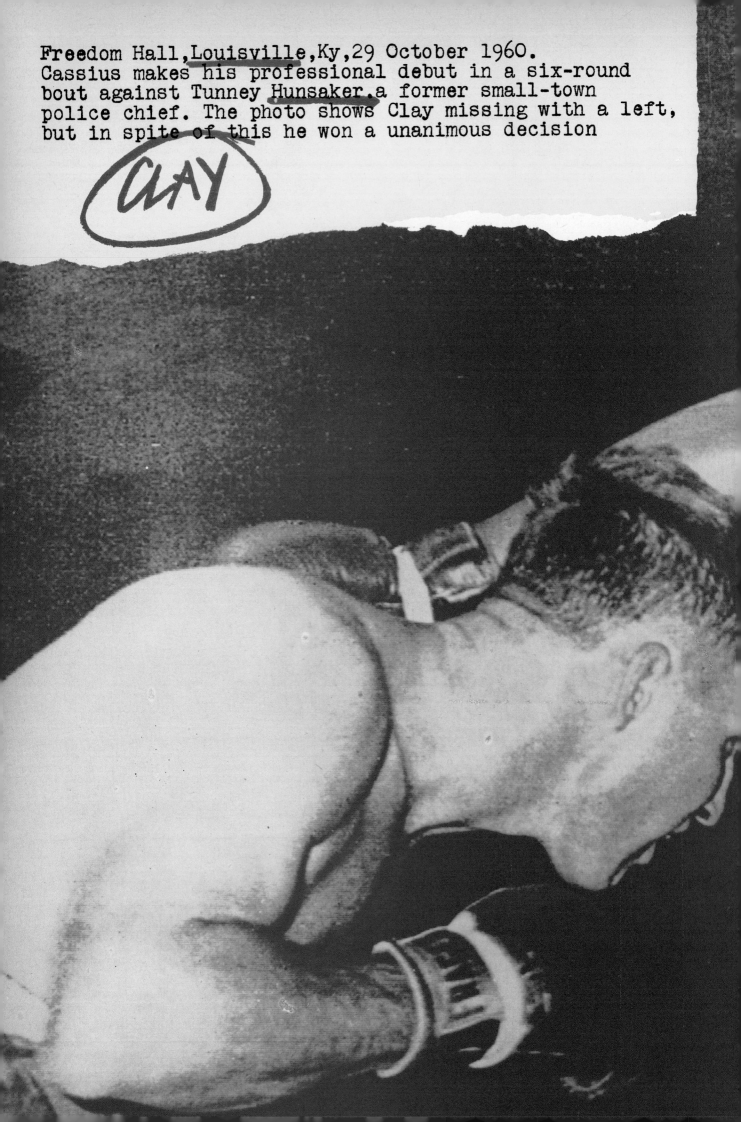

Freedom Hall,Louisville,Ky,29 October 1960.
Cassius makes his professional debut in a six-round
bout against Tunney Hunsaker,a former small-town
police chief. The photo shows Clay missing with a left,
but in spite of this he won a unanimous decision

CLAY

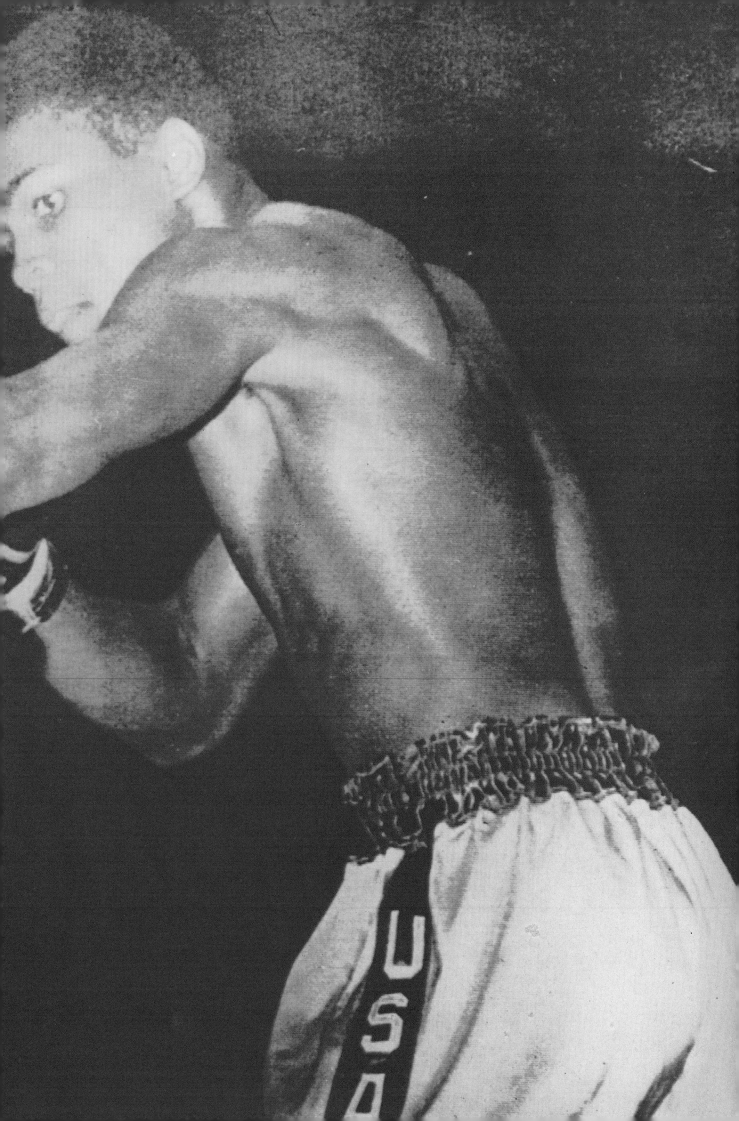

Louisville, Ky, 19/4/61. Down goes Lamar Clark, kayoed by Cassius in the second round. It was his fifth straight knock-out victory

CLAY v CLARK

Louisville, Ky, 7/10/61. Alex Miteff reels back under the Clay attack in the sixth round in which the Argentinian was clobbered to the mat for a TKO

CLAY v MITEFF

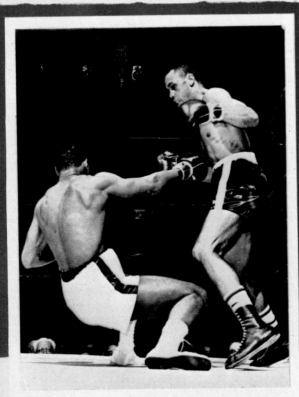

New York, N.Y., 10/2/62. A rare sight. Clay is decked in the first round by Sonny Banks at Madison Square Garden. Cassius fought back and stopped him in the fourth. Bill Faversham afterwards apologized to Bank's manager, a friend, who replied, 'It's nobody's fault, Sonny shouldn't have hit Clay in the first place.'

CLAY v BANKS

Los Angeles, Calif., 23/4/62. Cassius made it 13 victories straight when he stopped George Logan of Boise, Idaho in the fourth round of their scheduled ten-rounder. Photo shows Clay clipped in the first round

LOGAN

New York, N.Y., 19/5/62. Dr Sam Swetnick gives
Cassius and Billy Daniels their pre-fight examination.
Both fighters were undefeated professionally
until Clay inflicted a savage cut over Daniels's left eye
to end the fight in the seventh

CLAY V DANIELS

Los Angeles, Calif., 20/7/62. 'I will demolish this tall
man from Argentina in the fifth round,' said Cassius,
and that's exactly what he did. According to
Bill Faversham, he meted out such punishment as to
finish Alejandro Lavorante's fight career

LAVORANTE

Los Angeles, Calif., 15/11/62. 'Moore must fall in four,'
and Cassius knocked Archie down three times in
the predicted round. The ref awarded it to Clay without
even bothering to count. The late George Whiting of
the London *Evening Standard:* 'A fight? I would hardly
call it that. More like a massacre of an old man by
a supremely confident and almost contemptuous youth.'

MOORE

Pittsburgh, Pa., 24/1/63. Clay made it 17 out of 17
when he kayoed ex-footballer Charlie Powell in the third.
It was the third time in a row that he had called
the correct round on his opponent

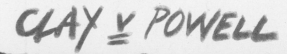

CLAY V POWELL

One of the toughest fights of Clay's whole career took place against Doug Jones at New York's Madison Square Garden on the night of 13 March 1963. Cassius had boasted that he would put away Jones, who was ranked fourth best in the world, in the fourth round. But according to *Boxing International*, 'For the first time in his professional career, Clay had to fight not to win, but to keep from losing. The crowd was hysterical. Dundee was screaming at a dazed Clay, "Grab him Cass! Hold on!"' After ten rounds of fistic fury, the judges awarded Cassius a unanimous decision and the crowd booed for more than five minutes

BOXING
NEWS ANNUAL

*
1964
RECORD
BOOK
*

7/6

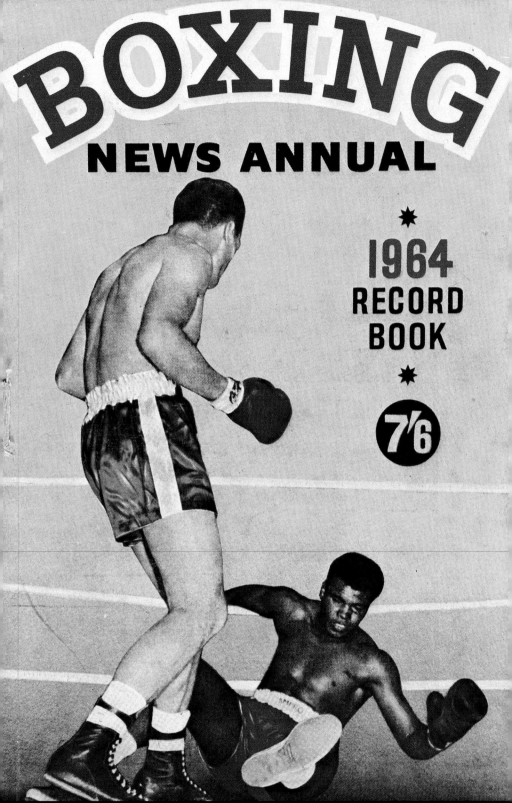

The first fight against Henry Cooper, Britain's best loved sportsman, took place in June 1963 a
Wembley Stadium, London. Bill Faversham said, 'Somebody had the poor taste to buy Clay a
crown which he wore into the ring. It was all rather embarrassing.' Cassius shocked the crowd with
'You gotta Queen, you need a King, I am King!' The 'King' crashed to the canvas in the fourth roun
nder the weight of 'enery's 'ammer', the left hook, but was up at four and saved by the bel
ngelo Dundee: 'Me cut Ali's glove after Cooper knocked him down? It just happened to be spli
ight? We killed about five or six minutes looking for new gloves. They didn't have no gloves
Iowever, a dreadful cut over Cooper's left eye ended it all in the fifth. Afterwards Ali said, 'Coope
as great, the toughest yet, he is no longer a bum.' The way was cleared for Charles 'Sonny' Listo

The Heavyweight Championship of the World, 25 February 1964, Miami Beach, Florida. After all the pre-fight publicity, Liston is totally out-psyched as shown in this photo from the sixth round. *Ring Magazine* reported, 'An easy target for Liston, he had been called. A fighter with a style unorthodox who would be punched full of holes, the dopesters had insisted. The fight destroyed the image of Liston's invincibility. The clay feet were exposed as belonging not to Cassius but to the slow, lumbering 218-pound fighter who had twice stopped Floyd Patterson in the first round.' The 'Great Ugly Bear' with the 15½″ fists, 7-1-on favourite, had failed to get off his stool at the start of the seventh round, due to an injured tendon in his biceps. Cassius was Champ

April 1964

50 Cents
P.D.C.

The RING

BIG
CHAMPIONSHIP
ISSUE

"I AM KING"

Immediately after the title fight, Cassius announced that he had joined the Black Muslims and was renouncing his slave name 'Clay'. It was a massive turning point in his life. Boxing was run exclusively by Whites, and the upsurge of Black consciousness in America in the 1960s terrified them. Middle America found it tough, if not impossible, to take the idea of a Black Muslim Champion. Right: Muhammad Ali addresses a Black Muslim Convention in Chicago, with his leader, Elijah Muhammad

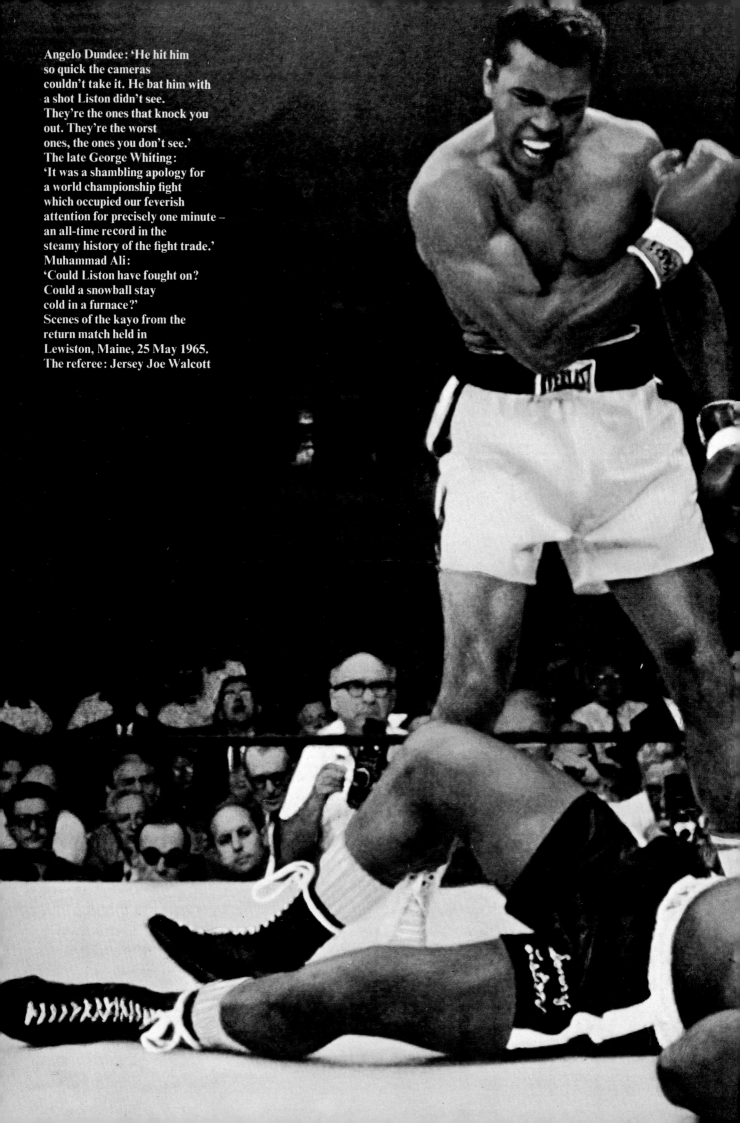

Angelo Dundee: 'He hit him
so quick the cameras
couldn't take it. He bat him with
a shot Liston didn't see.
They're the ones that knock you
out. They're the worst
ones, the ones you don't see.'
The late George Whiting:
'It was a shambling apology for
a world championship fight
which occupied our feverish
attention for precisely one minute –
an all-time record in the
steamy history of the fight trade.'
Muhammad Ali:
'Could Liston have fought on?
Could a snowball stay
cold in a furnace?'
Scenes of the kayo from the
return match held in
Lewiston, Maine, 25 May 1965.
The referee: Jersey Joe Walcott

The 'Sour Bear' looms dazed in the background during the post-fight pandemonium. Ali had stood over him during the count, yelling at him to get up and fight, but the challenge was ended. Bundini and Angelo are jubilant

Las Vegas,Nevada,22 November 1965. Champion Muhammad
Ali crashes a right into Floyd Patterson's head
during their scheduled 15-rounder. Ali TKO'd Floyd
in the 12th. Referee Harry Krause takes up the story:
'I said,"Man-to-man,Floyd,are you OK? Do you really
want to go on?" He said,"Yes please." It was hurting
me to watch, Patterson was hopelessly outclassed.
He lobbed his punches like a feeble old woman.'

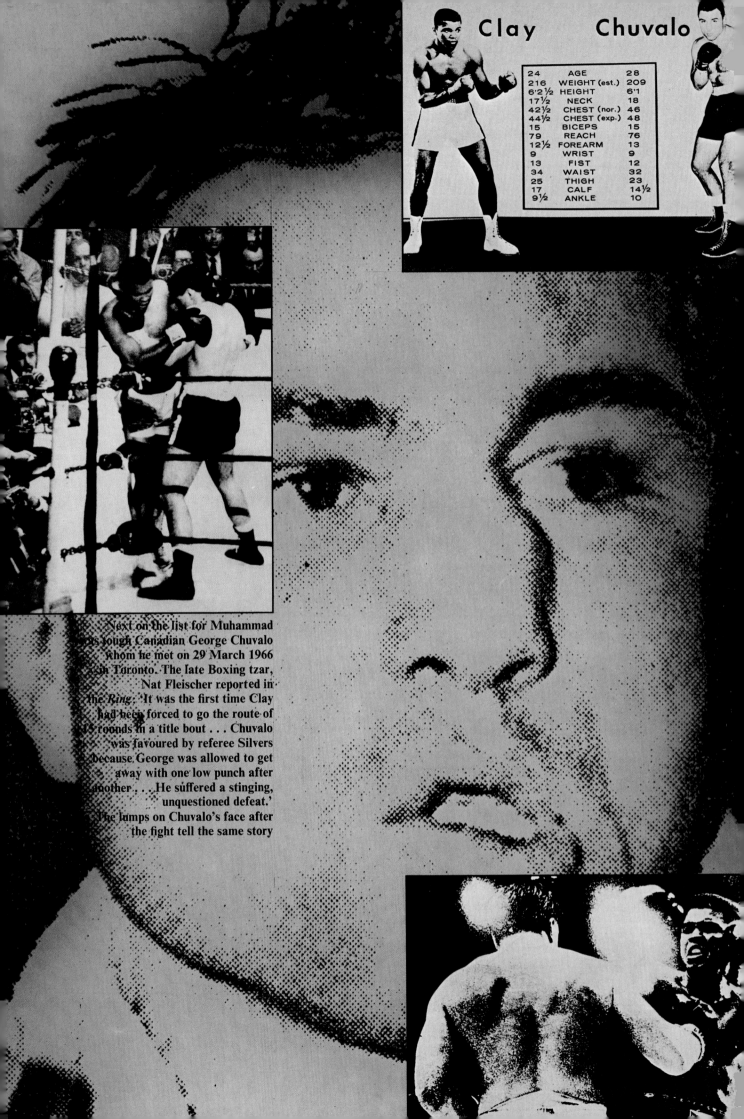

Clay   Chuvalo

Clay		Chuvalo
24	AGE	28
216	WEIGHT (est.)	209
6'2½	HEIGHT	6'1
17½	NECK	18
42½	CHEST (nor.)	46
44½	CHEST (exp.)	48
15	BICEPS	15
79	REACH	76
12½	FOREARM	13
9	WRIST	9
13	FIST	12
34	WAIST	32
25	THIGH	23
17	CALF	14½
9½	ANKLE	10

Next on the list for Muhammad
is tough Canadian George Chuvalo
whom he met on 29 March 1966
in Toronto. The late Boxing tzar,
Nat Fleischer reported in
the *Ring*: 'It was the first time Clay
had been forced to go the route of
15 rounds in a title bout . . . Chuvalo
was favoured by referee Silvers
because George was allowed to get
away with one low punch after
another . . . He suffered a stinging,
unquestioned defeat.'
The lumps on Chuvalo's face after
the fight tell the same story

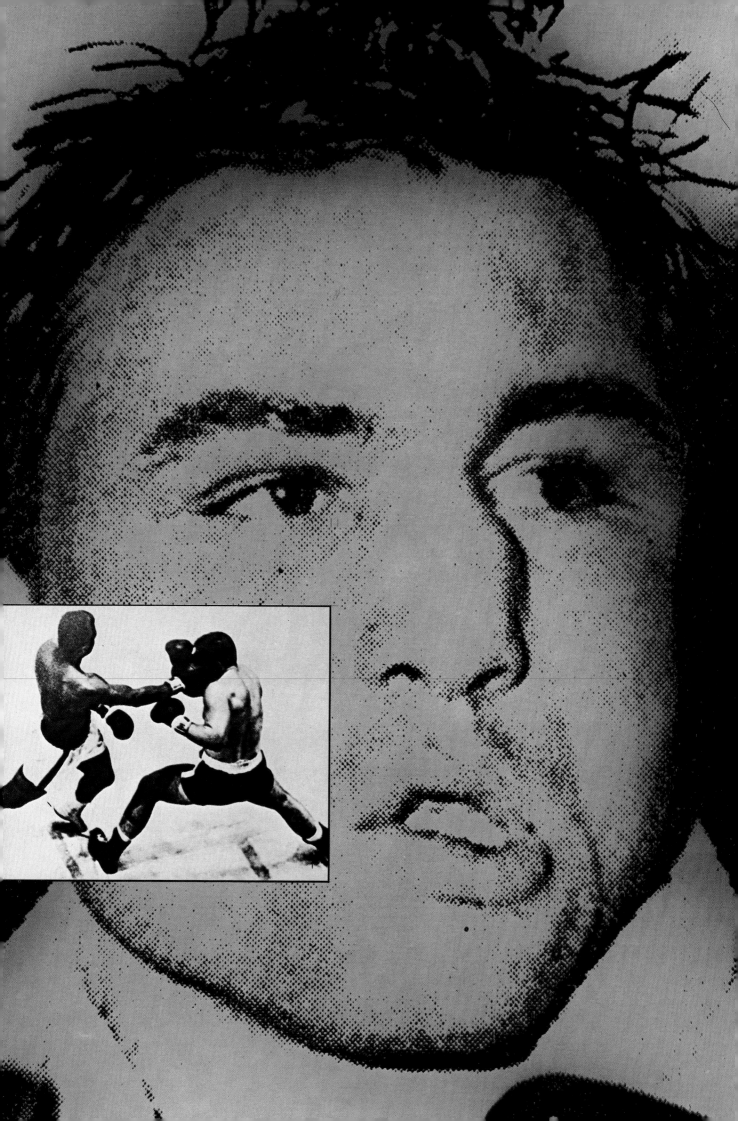

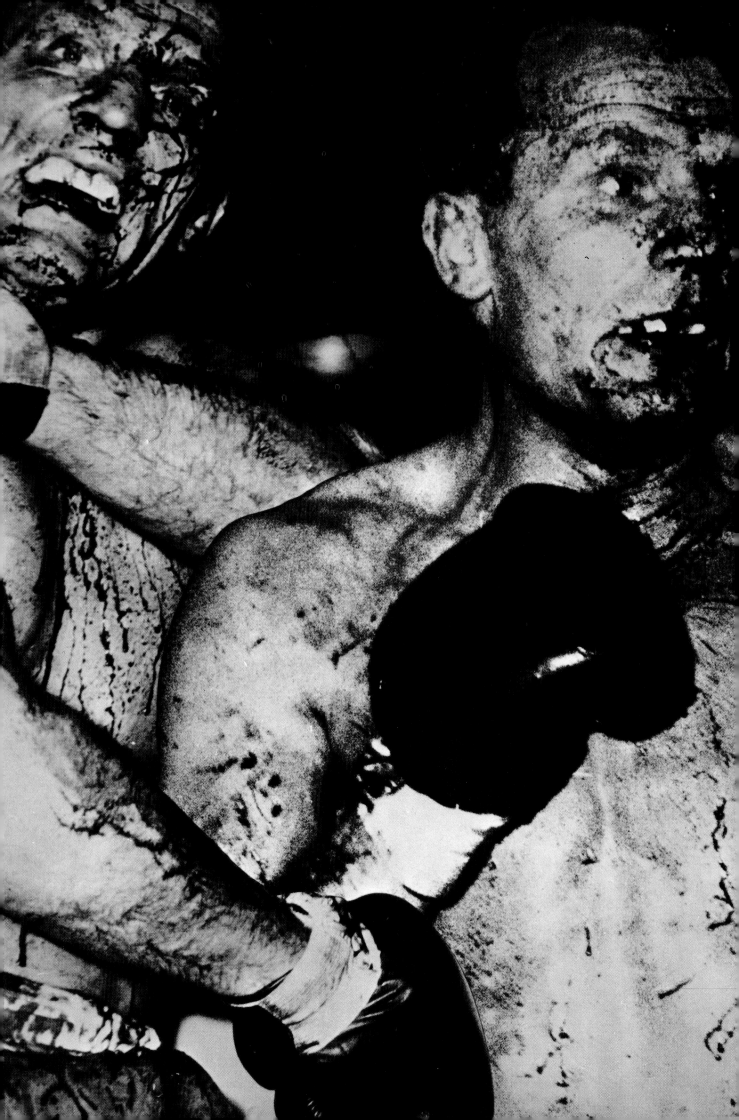

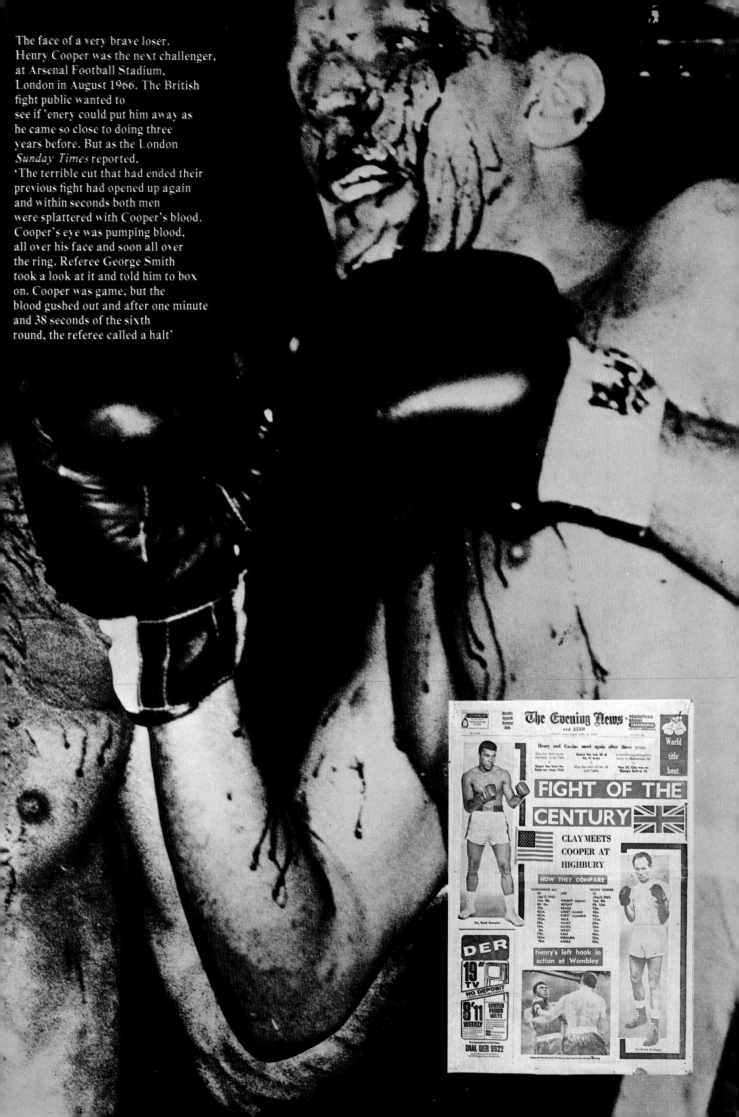

The face of a very brave loser.
Henry Cooper was the next challenger,
at Arsenal Football Stadium,
London in August 1966. The British
fight public wanted to
see if 'enery could put him away as
he came so close to doing three
years before. But as the London
Sunday Times reported,
'The terrible cut that had ended their
previous fight had opened up again
and within seconds both men
were splattered with Cooper's blood.
Cooper's eye was pumping blood,
all over his face and soon all over
the ring. Referee George Smith
took a look at it and told him to box
on. Cooper was game, but the
blood gushed out and after one minute
and 38 seconds of the sixth
round, the referee called a halt'

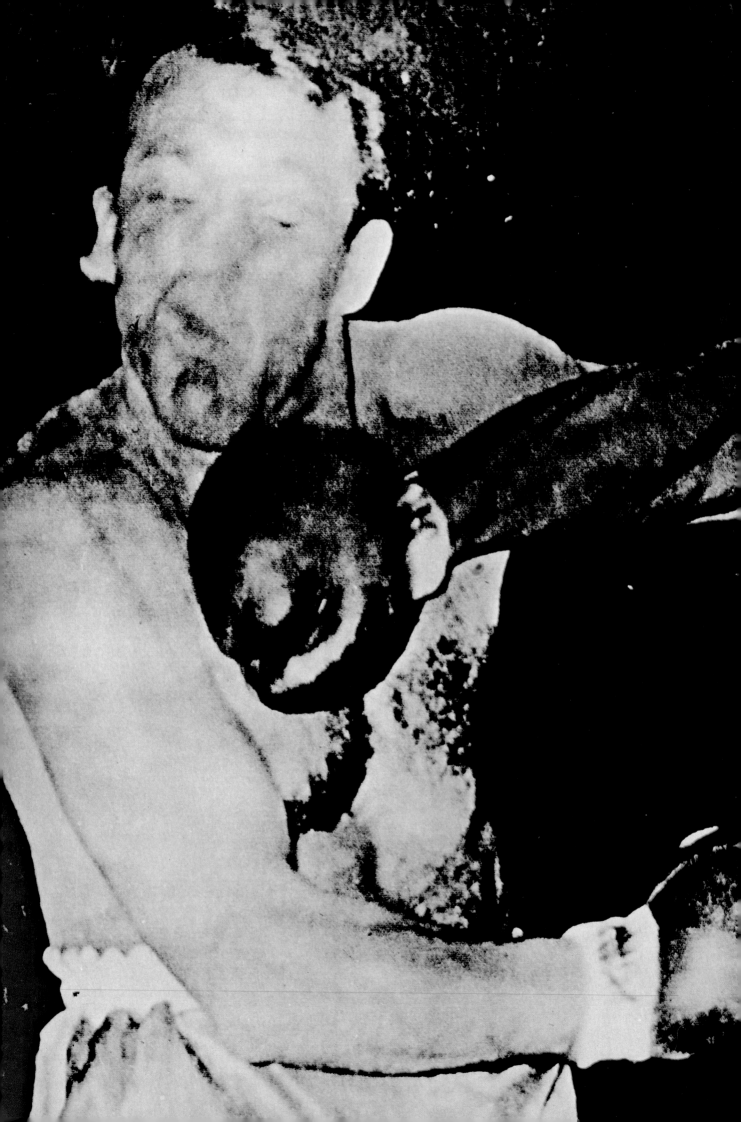

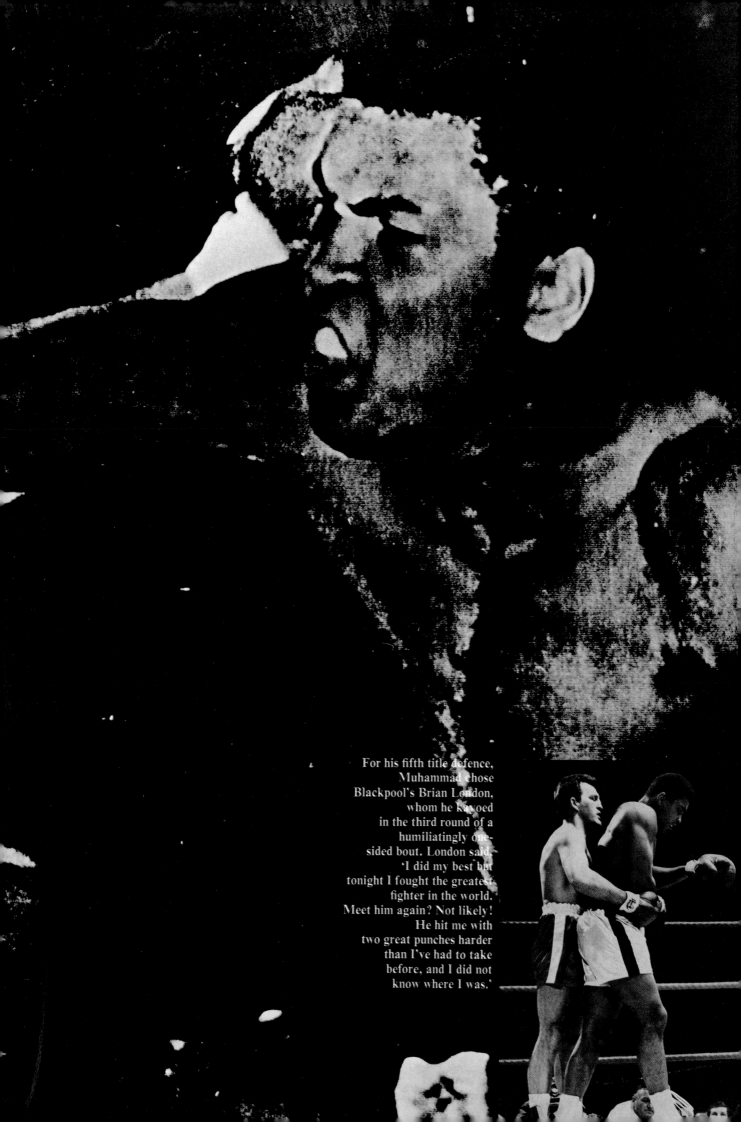

For his fifth title defence, Muhammad chose Blackpool's Brian London, whom he kayoed in the third round of a humiliatingly one-sided bout. London said, 'I did my best but tonight I fought the greatest fighter in the world. Meet him again? Not likely! He hit me with two great punches harder than I've had to take before, and I did not know where I was.'

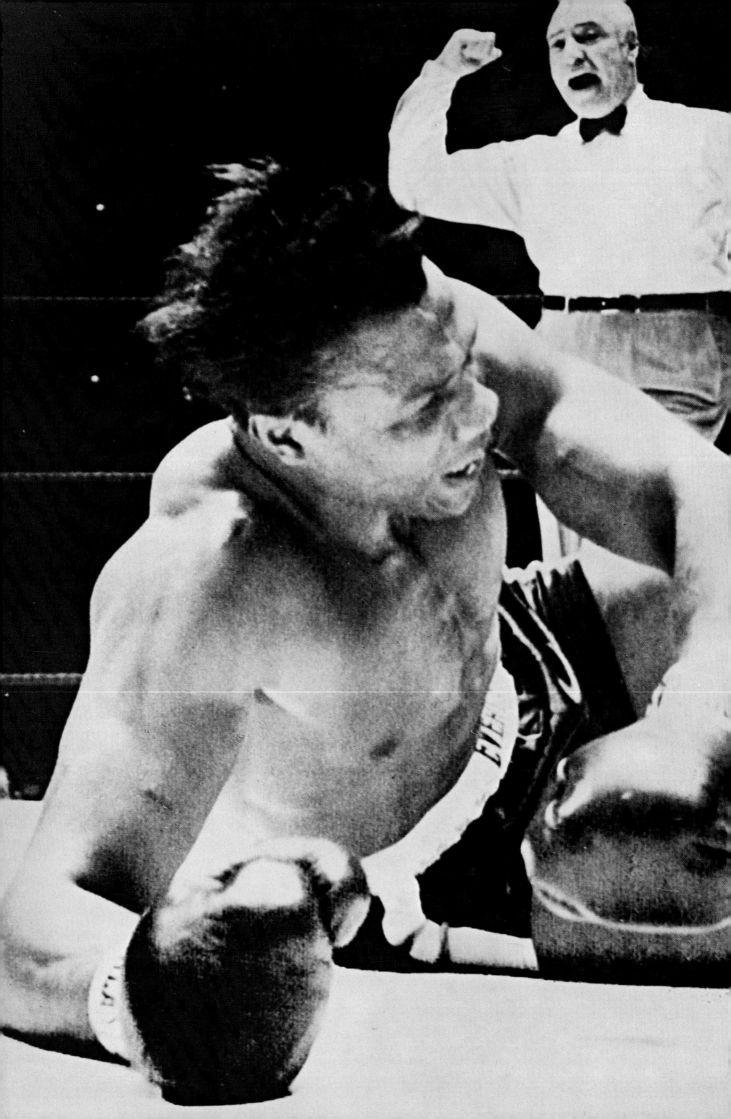

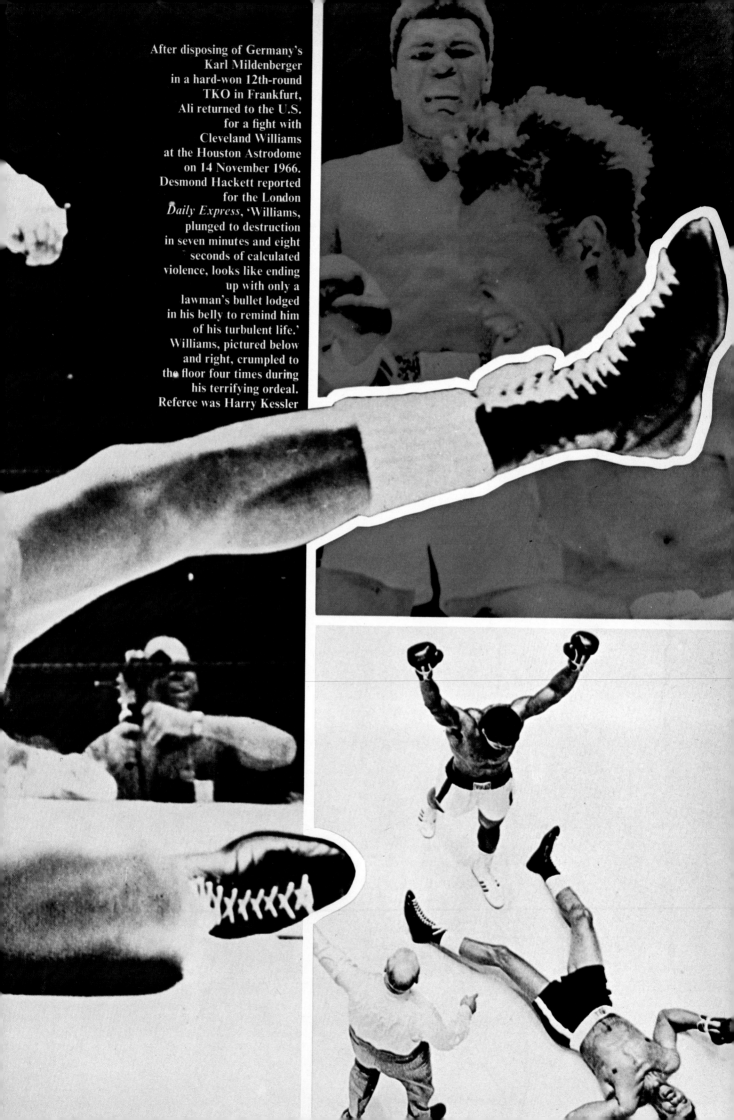

After disposing of Germany's Karl Mildenberger in a hard-won 12th-round TKO in Frankfurt, Ali returned to the U.S. for a fight with Cleveland Williams at the Houston Astrodome on 14 November 1966. Desmond Hackett reported for the London *Daily Express*, 'Williams, plunged to destruction in seven minutes and eight seconds of calculated violence, looks like ending up with only a lawman's bullet lodged in his belly to remind him of his turbulent life.' Williams, pictured below and right, crumpled to the floor four times during his terrifying ordeal. Referee was Harry Kessler

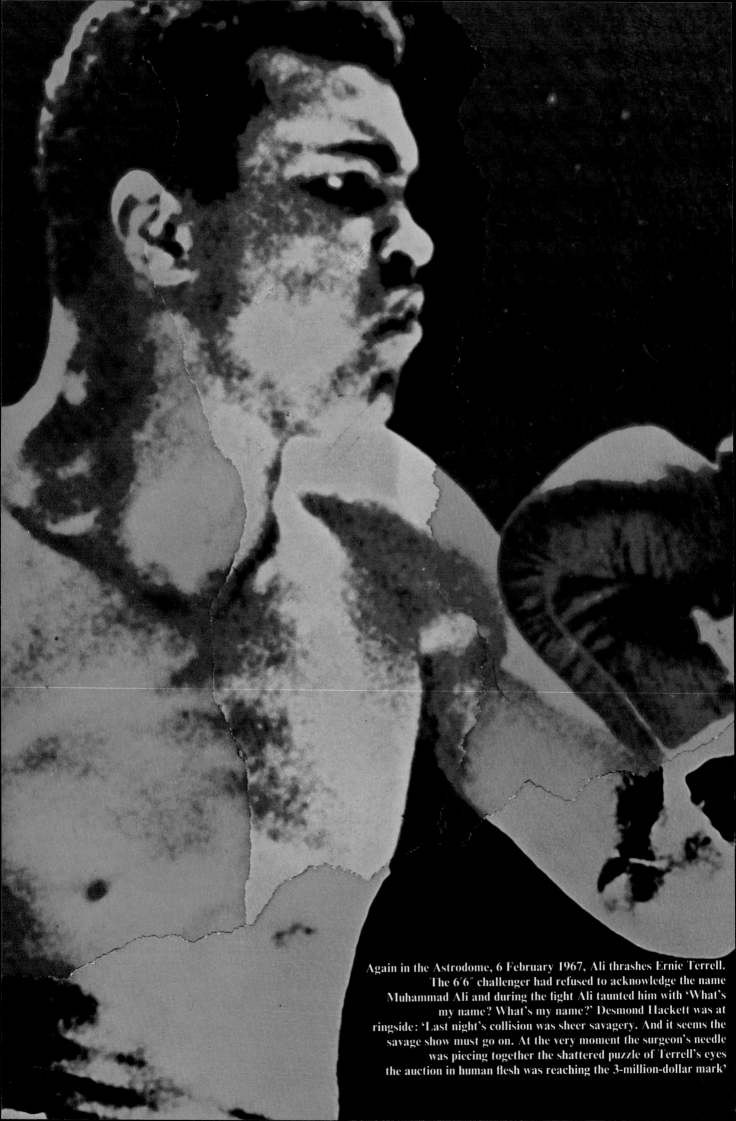

Again in the Astrodome, 6 February 1967, Ali thrashes Ernie Terrell. The 6′6″ challenger had refused to acknowledge the name Muhammad Ali and during the fight Ali taunted him with 'What's my name? What's my name?' Desmond Hackett was at ringside: 'Last night's collision was sheer savagery. And it seems the savage show must go on. At the very moment the surgeon's needle was piecing together the shattered puzzle of Terrell's eyes the auction in human flesh was reaching the 3-million-dollar mark'

Madison Square Garden on the night of 22 March 1967. The ninth and final title defence Muhammad was to make before the author took away his right to box. Zora Folley was the challenger. The late George Whiting: 'Those punches travelled no more than disastrous inches, but they exploded on Folley's luckless chin with a force that would have inconvenienced an ox. Folley crashed downward with a mighty thump, his nose buried in the boards, his quivering legs stretched wide apart like he was doing the spli counted 17 of those jabs in less than half a minute and if they did not shift Folley bodily they certainly snapped his head back and

...hing to improve the shape or colour of his ...rmally aquiline nose.' The scenes above ... from the fourth round, but the show ...pped in the seventh, right, as the ref ...n LoBianco signals that it's all over

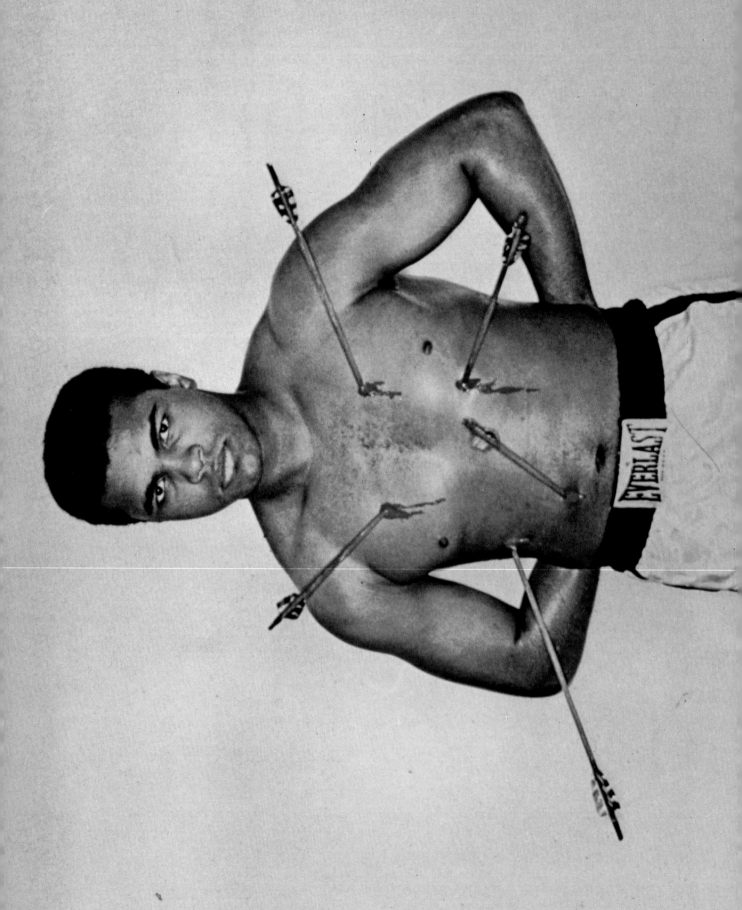

For the rest of 1967, and up until October 1970, Ali was refused the right to box, and had his Heavyweight crown taken away from him because he would not join the U.S. Armed Forces due to his Black Muslim beliefs. He had 'nothin' against no Viet Cong', and fought a long legal battle against a five-year jail sentence which was finally overturned 8 to 0 by the Supreme Court. He returned to the ring after his enforced lay off an even more legendary figure than before, and although overweight, whupped Jerry Quarry and outpointed Oscar Bonavena. But the official World Champion now was Joe Frazier and Muhammad wanted to 'sort out this whole heavyweight mess'

Ali and Frazier were both undefeated when they met at Madison Square Garden on the night of 8 March 1971, for what was rightly billed as the 'Fight of the Century'. Ali tried to lie on the ropes much of the time in the hope that Frazier would punch himself out but, 'He didn't get tired, you understand? He did NOT get tired!' Here Ali delivers a punishing right cross to Frazier's head

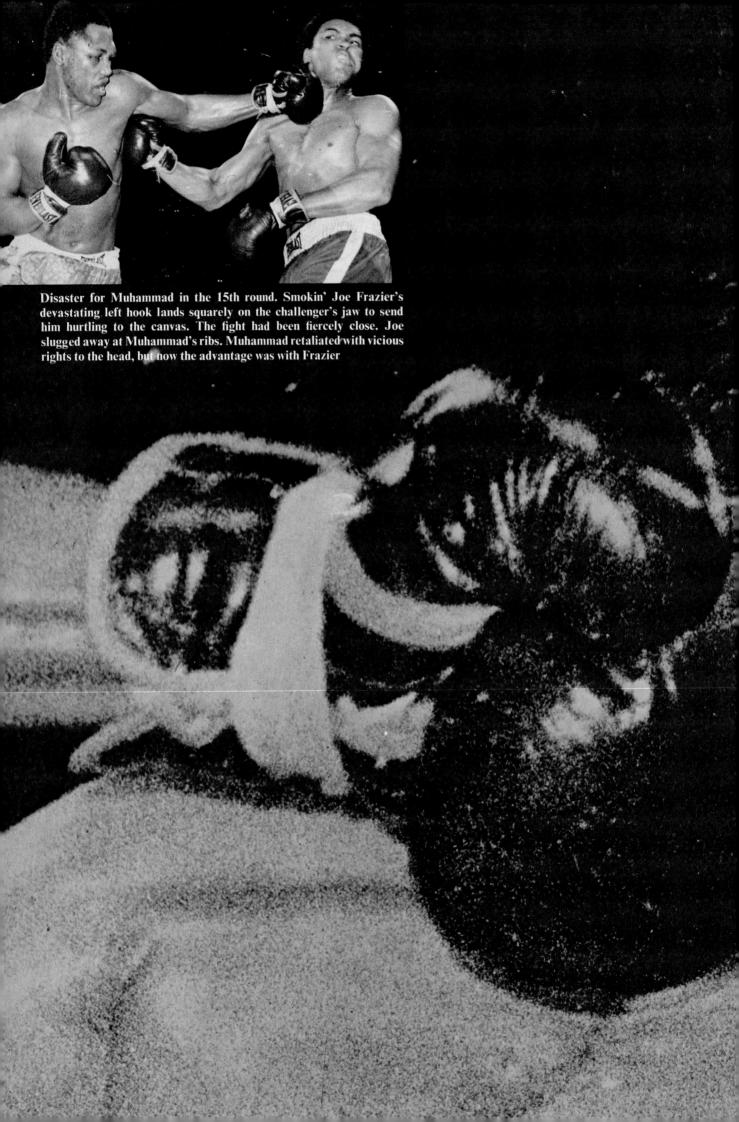

Disaster for Muhammad in the 15th round. Smokin' Joe Frazier's devastating left hook lands squarely on the challenger's jaw to send him hurtling to the canvas. The fight had been fiercely close. Joe slugged away at Muhammad's ribs. Muhammad retaliated with vicious rights to the head, but now the advantage was with Frazier

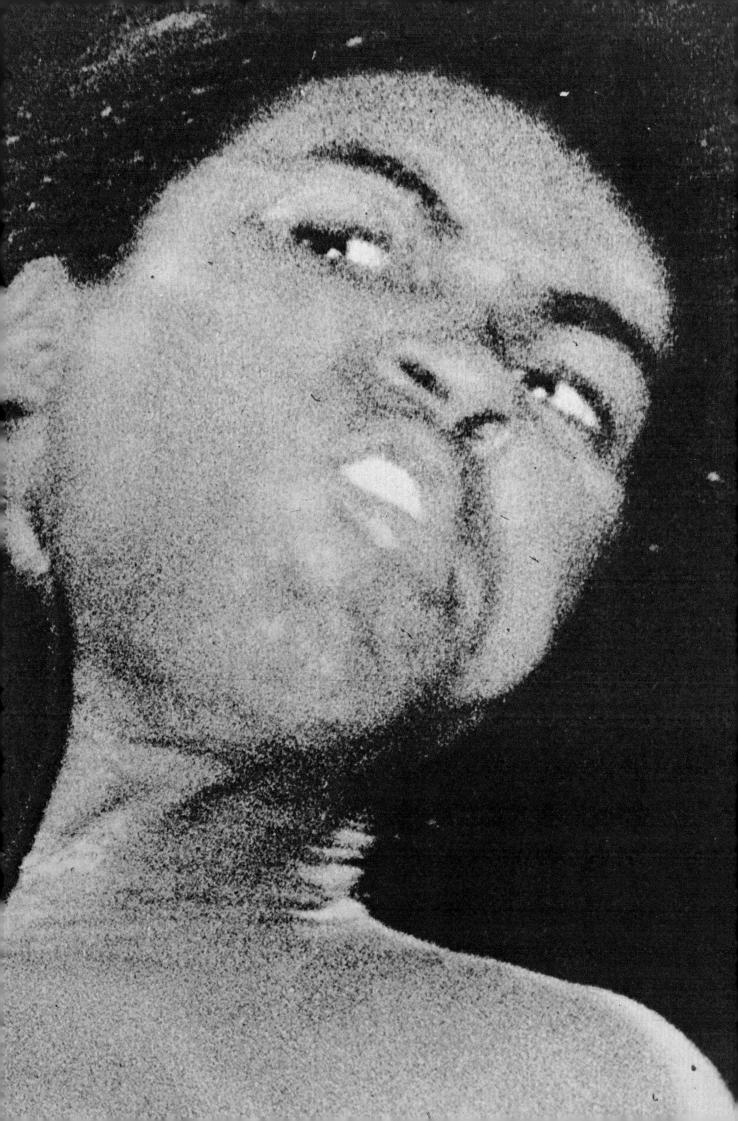

Muhammad was dumped for a count of eight, his jaw massively swollen. But he fought back strongly and by the end, Joe's eyes were almost invisible behind the super-accurate results of Muhammad's left jabs. Joe won the unanimous decision but he had to go into hospital after the fight. In defeat Ali simply said, 'I'm not going to cry.' His loss, far from diminishing his legend, actually strengthened his fans' affection and respect. Now the People's Champion was born

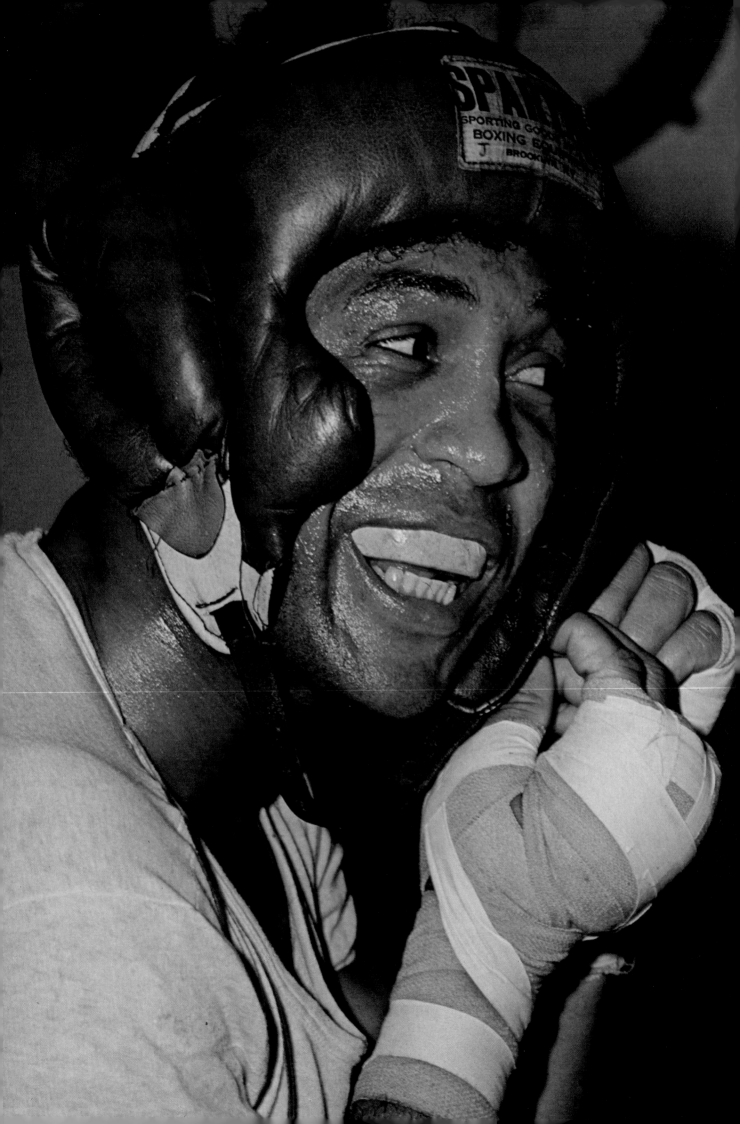

After a four-and-a-half-month rest, Ali started on the long road back to the Championship with a 12th-round TKO against Jimmy Ellis, his old sparring partner. Above: Ellis, left, and Cassius in training with friend back in their amateur days. Inset: Muhammad and Ellis trade leather in the seventh round. Opposite page: Ellis in training today. A massive 256-pound Buster Mathis next dragged himself to the slaughter, thudding to the deck four times in the last two rounds. Over the next 12 months a line of six other hopefuls all suffered defeat at Ali's hands.

Floyd Patterson   Muhammad Ali

'TALE OF THE TAPE'

37	AGE	30
195	WEIGHT (est.)	216
6'	HEIGHT	6' 3"
16½	NECK	17
40	CHEST (nor.)	42
42	CHEST (exp.)	44½
14½	BICEPS	15
71	REACH	80
12	FOREARM	12½
6	WRIST	9
12¾	FIST	13
32½	WAIST	34
21½	THIGH	25
15½	CALF	17
9½	ANKLE	9½

Floyd Patterson, at 37 years old, takes an Ali left–right on the nose near the end of their bout at Madison Square Garden in September 1972. Muhammad TKO'd Floyd in seven with a lacerated eye. Ali received the first cut of his career when he kayoed Bob Foster later that year

Las Vegas, Nevada, 14 February 1973. European Heavyweight Champion Joe Bugner tangles up close with Ali, who was lavishly introduced as 'the World's Greatest Heavyweight'. *Ring* said, 'It was a tactical fight and Joe was a lieutenant matched against a 10-star general.' Ali won every round. But Muhammad had his mind on other matters. Frazier had suffered a crushing defeat in January from George Foreman, a new unbeaten Champion. He had been knocked down six times in less than two rounds, and Foreman loomed a terrible threat in the distance. But first there was a fight against Ken Norton. Ken who? . . .

. . . Ken Norton, that's who, the 'fighting marine', and he bust Ali's jaw (X-ray) in the first round of their fight in San Diego, California on 31 March 1973. With the tremendous pain, Ali did well to survive the 12-round contest. Below: Ali and Bundini leave the disaster area after the fight. A rematch was held in September. Ali won on a split decision

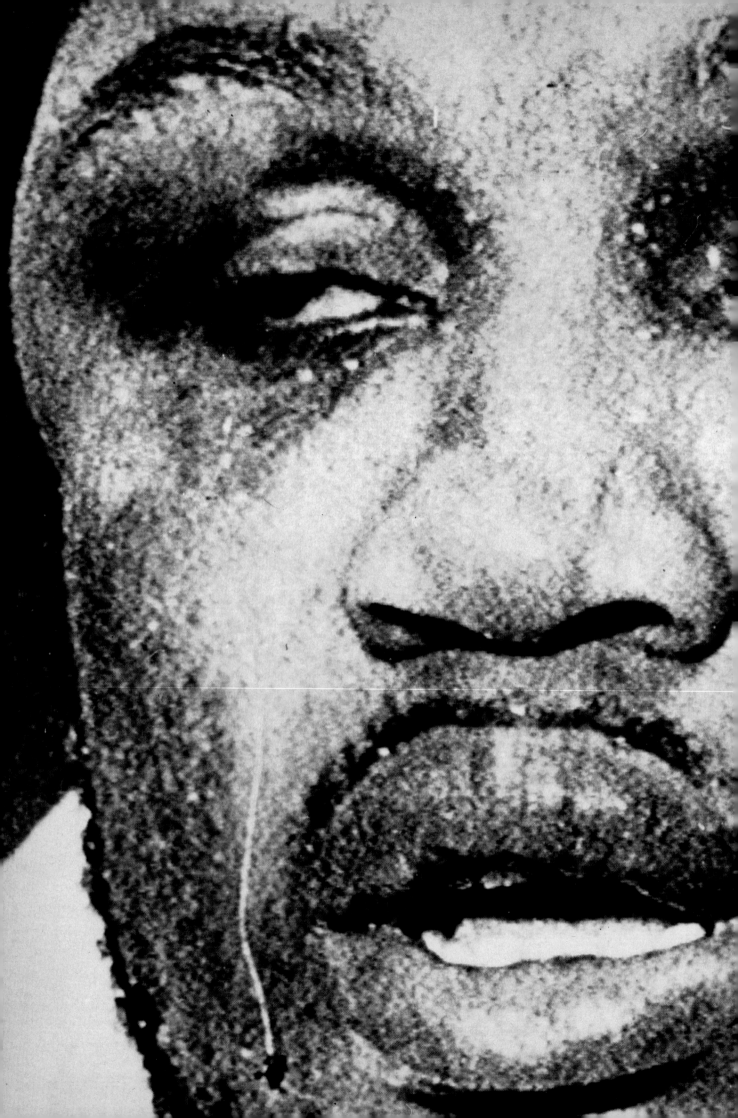

his second ... with Ali in Madison
... 1974. Another ... tough fight but this time
... down to business ... won the outright decision

'I'm gonna beat your Christian ass, you white flagwaving bitch you!'
A reference from Ali to Foreman waving the Stars
and Stripes both figuratively and literally. But before he could do it,
he would have to train like he'd never trained before

Ali's camp in the Pennsylvania Mountains. Inset: Ali training in his gym.
The former champions' names were painted on the rocks by Cassius Clay Sr

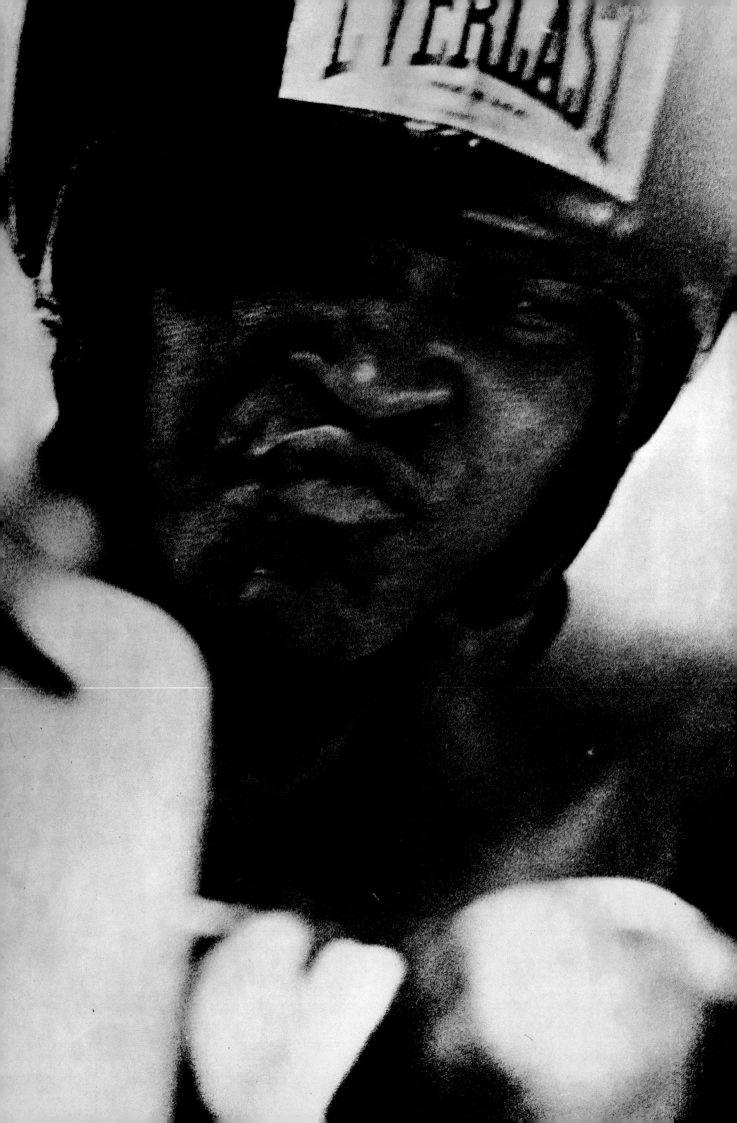

'This fight I'm gonna get it all out'

This interview with Muhammad Ali took place at his camp in the Pennsylvania Mountains before he went to Zaire for the Foreman fight. The photographs show him in training

It's the press, the press. They've been spreading all these rumours around about me. That my legs have gone, that I'm old, I'm finished, I ain't got no strong punch and pretty soon they had George Foreman believing it; but when he hears the referee calling out, 'Round six, round seven, round eight,' is he gonna be surprised!

Sometimes I wish he was a tree and I was a dog. When he was a little kid he wanted to box but they couldn't find a mouthpiece big enough for him, he's so ugly. This fight is going to be the biggest shock in history. They said I couldn't beat Liston. They hated me joining the Muslims. I had that trouble with the Army. Well, I'm still here. Foreman don't scare me, he don't hit hard. Foreman's gonna be scared of me, 'cos he gonna think I'm crazy 'cos I know he don't hit hard.

> I've got speed, power and endurance,
> and any one who fights me
> had better take out extra life insurance.

Sonny Liston, he scared white people 'cos they all thought he was so ugly. And *you* think that George Foreman is ugly and he scares you. Because you all think the black men are ugly. But I'm not scared because I'm black and I don't think he's as ugly as you do.

Frazier and Norton – they can't punch 'cos they don't know how to punch. They can't dance 'cos they

don't know how to dance; they can't box, 'cos they don't know how to box; they can't think their way out of trouble 'cos they can't think and they can't even write poetry!

I'm the prettiest, look at me, and I've been fighting for 20 years. I'm serious, it's hard to be humble when you're as great as I am. Think of the money I've made for those guys. Nobody would go to see them if I wasn't fighting. I do it and they're collecting on it.

A fine champion is one who can make a difficult situation easy. Foreman is a difficult situation. I'm the people's Champion. You can walk right up to me and say 'Hallo' without paying. Try getting near to Frank Sinatra or Elvis. There no bodyguards around this camp.

If I lose this fight, I shall retire, no doubt. It will be a sad thing for boxing. The show will be over. But it's hard to give up when I just been offered $5,000,000 for another fight with Frazier. That's good money!

But I look so old now, look at these photographs of me. I ain't scared of nobody. That's why they think I'm mad. And that scares them. Like Malcolm X – they shot him and the papers said I was next on the list. But it didn't scare me.

You like the Lincoln? Why, thank you. I've got seven cars, two of them are Rolls-Royces, I've got a Jeep, a Volkswagen bus. But they've all got a purpose, I haven't got seven just for the sake of it. This one's great for meeting people at the airport. [His white Lincoln Continental is equipped with two telephones, colour TV, stereo tape-deck and a digital clock.]

Fred Stoner trained me from the age of 13 to 17. I went to Joe Martin's gym from 8 to 10 and then on to

Fred Stoner's from 10.30 to midnight. Joe Martin was good for publicity. I had my first fight on his TV show at the age of 12. That's when I first knew I'd be the Champion of the whole world. I beat a guy called Ronnie O'Keefe on a split decision.

Fred Stoner had more boxing science. He had a better training programme. It was left jab, left jab, left jab and move, jab, jab, jab and move. Discipline? We kept strict discipline on ourselves down there. Stoner said my brother could have been better than me? Could have been. But Elvis has brothers and they can't sing. And there were other guys at that time and they never made it. After this fight I'm gonna give Fred Stoner a few thousand dollars, just for himself, I don't forget people.

I felt good after sparring. I need to lose some weight. I'm 226 now, and I want to come down to around 215.

Maybe I won't have to go 15 rounds, you can't tell. I've never been stopped but you can't just dance around all through the fight. Get too tired. You have to move in, tie them up. I shouldn't get caught in the ropes, but you can't always tell.

Life is a gamble, you can get hurt, but people die in plane crashes, lose their arms and legs in car accidents, people die everyday. Same with fighters. Some die, some get hurt, some go on. You just don't let yourself believe it will happen to you. You get used to being hit, you condition yourself. It doesn't hurt me mostly.

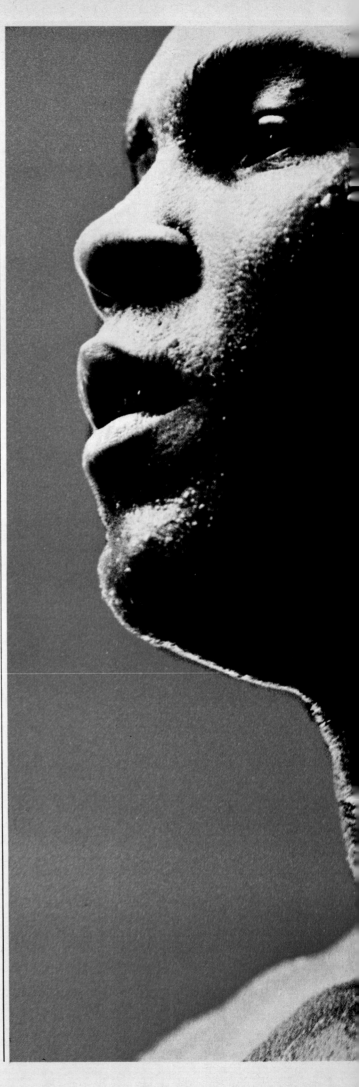

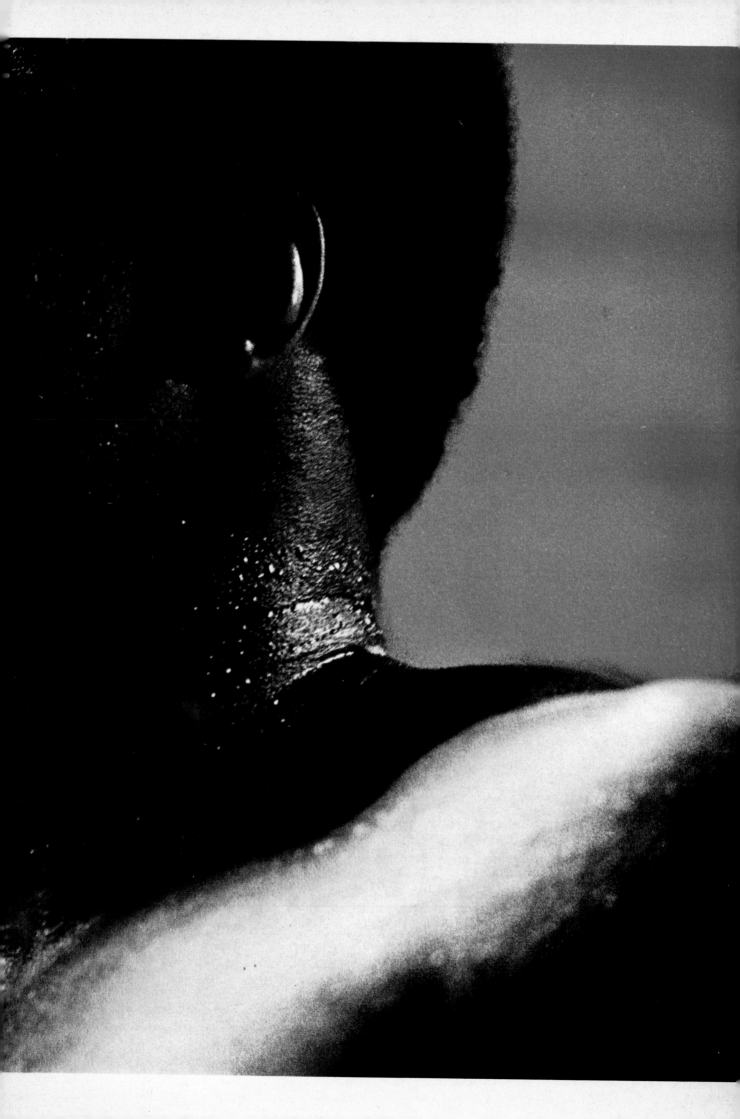

It's a disadvantage not wanting to hurt your opponent. Like when I hurt Cooper. But I'm cutting out this business for Foreman. This fight I'm gonna get it *all* out.

Death is the price that the soul has to pay, for having a name and a form.

Life is a fair trade. It all adjusts itself in time. For all that you take from it, you must pay the price sooner or later. For some things you may pay in advance. For some things you pay on delivery. And for others you pay when the bill is presented.

Fred Stoner taught me everything I know. Angelo got me when I was ready to make the money. They cashed in on it. Chris is a good promoter. Angelo is good to have at the fight. But I have my own style. Nobody in-

The People's Champion with the Champion's grin

fluenced me after Fred Stoner. It wasn't tough in Louisville when I was a kid, I started fighting because I liked it. The publicity, the glamour, the trips. I was fighting on Joe Martin's TV show when George Foreman was still in his diapers.

I don't hate Foreman. I don't hate no one. I don't even hate whites. That was in history, but it's coming to an end. Elijah Muhammad tells us that hate causes frustration. We Muslims hate injustices and evil but we don't have time to hate people. White people wouldn't be here if God didn't mean them to be. If a rattlesnake comes in my room, I keep away from it. That doesn't mean I hate snakes.

People come to the camp every day to see me. After 3.30 I give them an hour or two. I like to see people.

I'm buying a 16-room house in Chicago. Half a block from Elijah Muhammad, the greatest black man to ever walk the Earth. He's our leader.

I was brought up a Christian, I used to go to a Christian church till I was about 16. The only people who go there are the very young and the very old. Black people know what the Christian ministers say isn't true.

One day in Florida some people in the street invited me in to a Muslim meeting at Temple 29 in Miami. I believed everything they said and I joined the same night. Since then I've been welcomed in every Muslim country on Earth. Countries that don't welcome Christians. In America we recognize whites as slave-drivers and lynchers. There's no way they could be comfortable in

our presence. We won't have them at our meetings.

We believe what is said in the Bible, but not the King James's translation. He was a homosexual. There are no homosexuals in the Black Muslims. If we found any we'd throw them out. But the American way of life causes people to be promiscuous, prostitutes, drug addicts . . . We try to convert them but they still have these traits. If you're born a Muslim, you don't do any of these things.

Elijah Muhammad is so wise, no one can challenge us. We have our own farms, our hospital, we have our own everything. He's now importing 50,000,000 fish a week from Peru. He did a deal with the government there.

What other boxer has built their own camp? I've done this. You can see it's clean, there's no smoking, good food. It don't smell. People dress properly. This is just a small manifestation of his teachings.

Did you see the film, *The Ten Commandments*? Moses put an 'X' on the door of all the people who had been saved. This is symbolic. That's why now Muslims have an 'X' in their names. Moses was illiterate. Could hardly speak. Elijah Muhammad is the Moses of this day. We know that America, that's North America, not even Canada, is going to be destroyed if black people aren't freed. The English, you've been freed; the French, the new African countries. Now it's our turn. And they've got these UFOs up there just waiting to come down and blow it sky-high with bombs that go one-mile deep into the ground. I've got a film of them, someone from Washington gave it to me.

With the first Frazier fight I didn't respect him enough. I went in with the wrong attitude. Same with Norton. He didn't win that first fight, you know, I lost it. I was runnin' around, training in bars and expensive hotels. Not eating the right food and I went in the ring at 222.

But when you saw me come out the second time against Joe Frazier, you couldn't believe how pretty I looked! And I went in the ring at 212 which was the same weight that I fought Sonny Liston for the World's Heavyweight Championship all those years ago. And I danced for 12 whole rounds. Didn't I look pretty?

And people even came over all the way from England. They had no gas, no electricity, they were working on a three-day week, and they still found the money to come and see me whip Joe Frazier. 10,000,000 people watched that fight.

Ali greets President Mobuto of Zaire in Kinshasa, 1974. Foreman waves the flag at the Olympics in Mexico, 1968

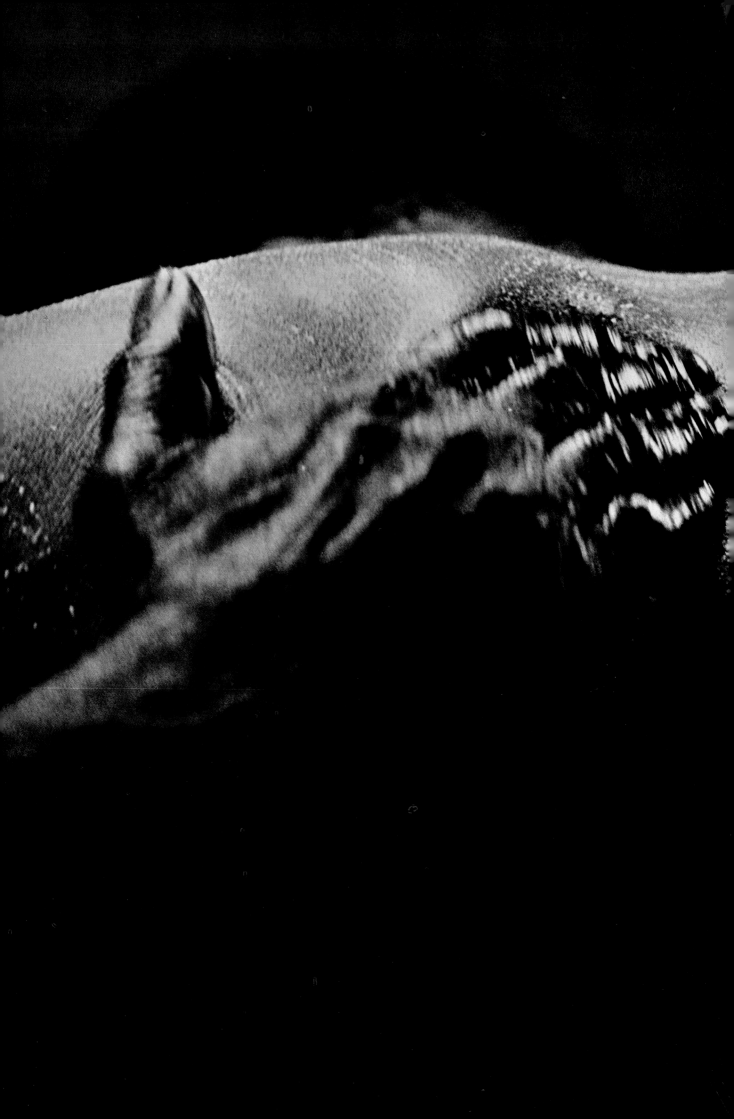

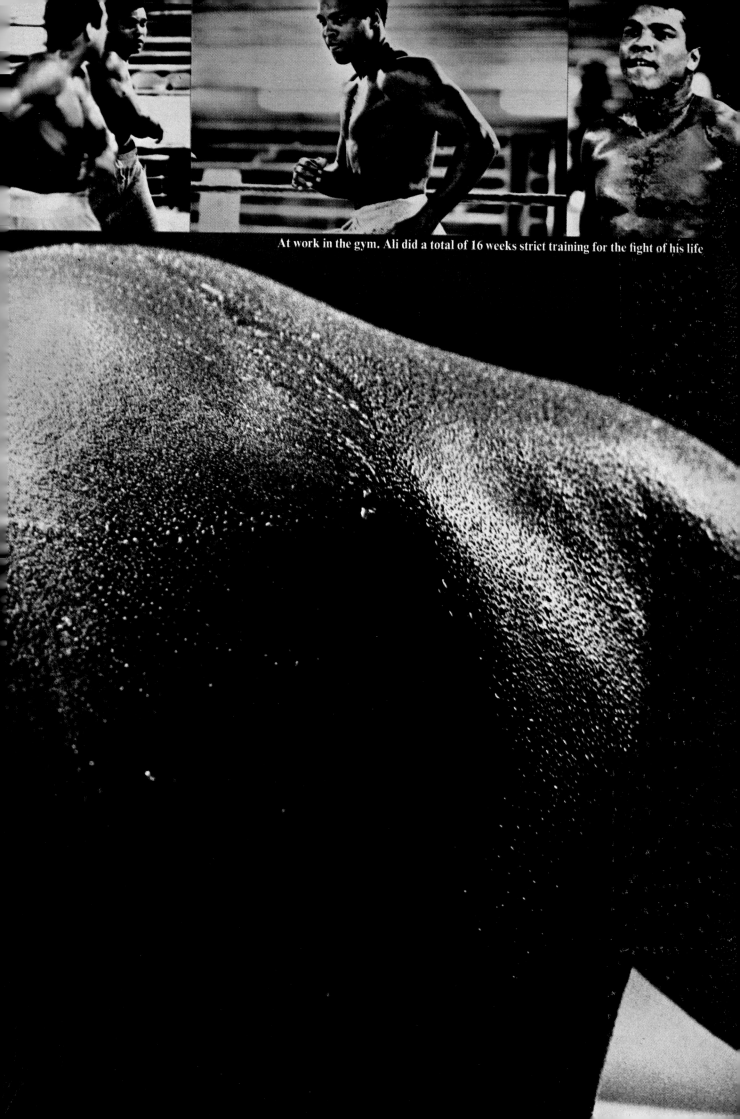

At work in the gym. Ali did a total of 16 weeks strict training for the fight of his life

'Clay's gonna come in like a billy-goat!'

Some predictions from Ali's associates on yet another Fight of the Century. None of them doubted he could win

Rahaman Ali He said to me when he was 12 that he wanted to do things no one ever did before. No fights have ever been in Africa. If he defeats George Foreman, I don't think he'll stop. He's intoxicated with success. He's only 32 years old; he has another few years. He will be joyful, Sir.

Against Foreman my brother will be underdog. He's 10 years older and fighting a tough opponent. His hands may be a bit brittle now, and he's a bit slower on his feet. Still – he can move. Foreman can't move. My brother's better now than when he beat Sonny Liston. He's stronger, got more wisdom. With Liston he hadn't experienced all this. Nothing can equal that Liston fight but this one with Foreman. With Liston it was my brother getting over the hump – he likes to do the impossible. When he beats Foreman it will be even greater. It has to do with a lot of things. It's a holy war. Foreman is a Christian. There are more Muslims in Africa than Christians so he'll be at home there. He always wanted to fight in Africa, that's why he suggested Zaire.

This fight will be greater to my brother than any fight. He is the People's Champion. Who would you rather be, the People's Champion or World Champion? When he beats Foreman he will be both! He fights better in hot weather. He sweats better in a hot climate.

I think Cassius has a pretty good chance of winning

Joe Martin I can't see him letting Foreman get that close to hurt him. It will be a pretty even fight.

this fight with Foreman. If he gets up not right that morning, he's had it. If he's right, he'll beat Foreman. You can get up with a slight pain in your stomach or not feeling as good as usual. It happens to us all, he's human. I can't see him letting Foreman get that close to hurt him. It will be a pretty even fight now because of their age difference. If they were the same age Foreman wouldn't stand a chance. Clay's gonna come in like a billy-goat!

Bill Faversham If he trains as hard for the Foreman fight as he did for his second fight with Frazier, he might out-dance Foreman. Foreman has been quite lazy since winning the championship. He might knock Cassius out, I hope not, he's never been knocked out.

I can see that Cassius is not hitting with his left any more, and he doesn't dance after a couple of rounds. But nothing overwhelms Cass, not even if he met God.

Fred Stoner He has the tools to take Foreman. Foreman's not a boxer, not fast. He's really rather clumsy but a terrific puncher. Clay's going to have to be in top condition. If he trains right, he's got what it takes. He'll have to go back to his old style. He has to keep on the move till the last bell goes. He's got to attend strictly to business. If he can carry him from six to eight rounds, then Foreman will be getting arm-weary, and Clay can go to work. I think Clay would be foolish to try to knock him down, he should go the 15 rounds.

I'm not going to Zaire. I'm needed here to give some of the other kids a chance to get where Clay is. Besides I've been watching him box, it's no different because it's the championship.

Ali said, 'If I lose this fight, I'll retire, no doubt...' This photograph shows him before he brought his weight down to a trimmer 216½. Right: the threatening features of George Foreman, who growled: 'He's gonna have to worry about getting hurt. I get my fights over with quick.' He did too, having won 37 of his 40 pro bouts inside the distance and gaining decisions on the other three. Of his last nine fights, eight had ended in the second round, the other in the first. In his last three, he had decked his opponents 10 times

FOREMAN		ALI
99,7 K	Weight	96,1 K
1,90 M	Height	1,90 M
24	Age	32
109,2 CM	Chest (norm.)	109,2 CM
115,5	Chest (exp.)	114,3
86,3	Waist	86,3
63,5	Thigh	66,0
31,7	Fist	33,0
44,4	Neck	44,4
40,6	Biceps	38,1
199,4	Reach	203,2

GEORGE FOREMAN

MUHAMMAD ALI

ZAIRE

Kinshasa

After a four-week delay due to Foreman suffering a cut eye in training, the $10-million bash ($5 million each) got under way at 2 a.m. 30 October 1974 in the 20th of May Stadium in Kinshasa, Zaire. Photo shows action in the seventh as Ali clubs Foreman with a stiff right

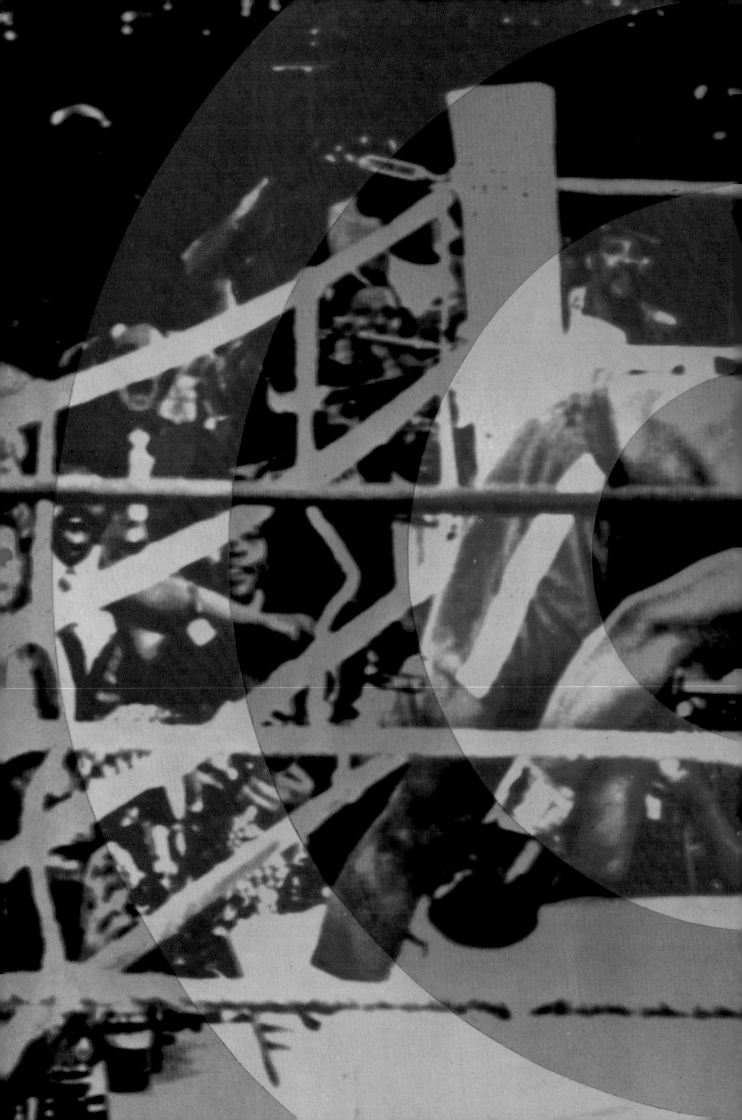

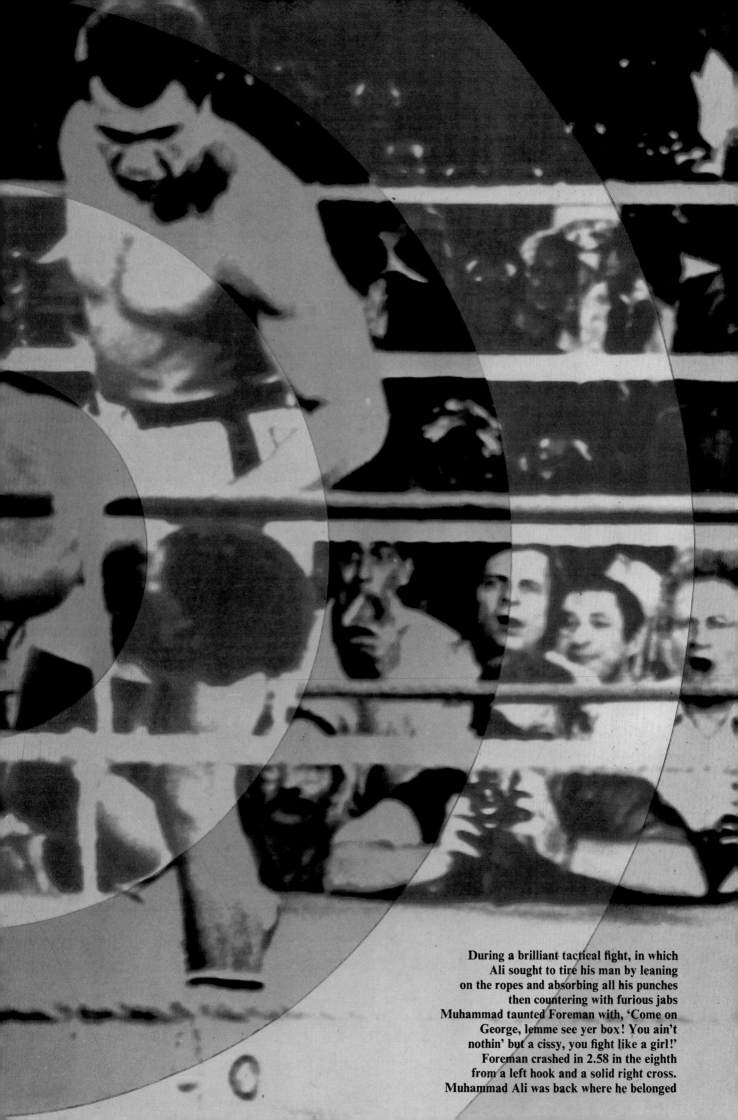

During a brilliant tactical fight, in which
Ali sought to tire his man by leaning
on the ropes and absorbing all his punches
then countering with furious jabs
Muhammad taunted Foreman with, 'Come on
George, lemme see yer box! You ain't
nothin' but a cissy, you fight like a girl!'
Foreman crashed in 2.58 in the eighth
from a left hook and a solid right cross.
Muhammad Ali was back where he belonged

'I am King'

Immediately after knocking out George Foreman, the 'Heavyweight Champion of the Whole Planet Earth' speaks

I kept telling him he has no power, I kept telling him he don't hit hard, and guess what he did in the end? He started fighting dirty. But I'm smart, I'm a pro see? I was good wasn't I? I was talking to him throughout the fight too. Ain't I the greatest of all time?

I proved that Allah is God, Elijah is his messenger. I have faith in him that regardless of the world and the pressure, I made it an easy fight, because Allah has power over all things. If you believe in him, even George Foreman gonna look like a baby. It wasn't a close fight was it?

Let everybody stop talking now – Attention!

I told you, all my critics, I told you all that I was the greatest of all time when I beat Sonny Liston. I'm still the greatest of all times. Never again say that I'm going to be defeated. Never again make me the under-dog. Until I'm about 50, then you might get me.

I didn't dance, I didn't dance for a reason. I wanted to make him lose all his power, I kept telling him that he has no punch, couldn't hit, swings like a sissy! He's missing! Let me see yer box! I hadn't started dancing yet. You can't say my legs was going, you can't say I was tired because what happened? I didn't dance from the second round on. I stayed on the ropes, and when I stay on the ropes you think I'm doing bad. I want all boxers to put this in the pages of boxing. Staying on the ropes is a beautiful thing with a heavyweight, when you make him shoot his best shots, and you know he's not hitting you. I gave George two rounds of steady punch-ing, because after that he was mine. He was falling, he was missing.

Thank the Almighty God Allah. I want all of you fans out there who believe in me, read the *Muhammad Speaks* newspaper, go to your local Muslim temple and learn more about the life-giving power from Allah through Elijah Muhammad, that I've got. You saw all the white people, the critics, the world had me ringed to go down. This was their man and Allah God was with me, and this man looked like nothing.

I told him he has no power, told him I'm going back to the ropes. Didn't I look stronger than him?

I was blocking, and I was pulling back. I have a radar built inside me to avoid George's punches. Didn't I tell all of you out there on your local radio – mostly black stations – I told you, 'I'm gonna float like a butterfly and sting like a bee, his hands can't hit what his eyes can't see.' So that's what happened.

They took my title unjustly. I told you I'm the real Champion! I told you I'm the Champion of the World. Bow ya'all bow. All of my critics, crawl! All of you suckers who write for boxing magazines, all of you suckers bow, because the stage is set! You made him great, you made him a bad George, you made him a hard puncher, but I want everybody from this moment on to recognize me as the styler of boxing! If you want to know any damn thing about boxing, don't go to no boxing experts in Las Vegas, don't go to no Jimmy the Greek, come to Muham-mad Ali! I am the man!

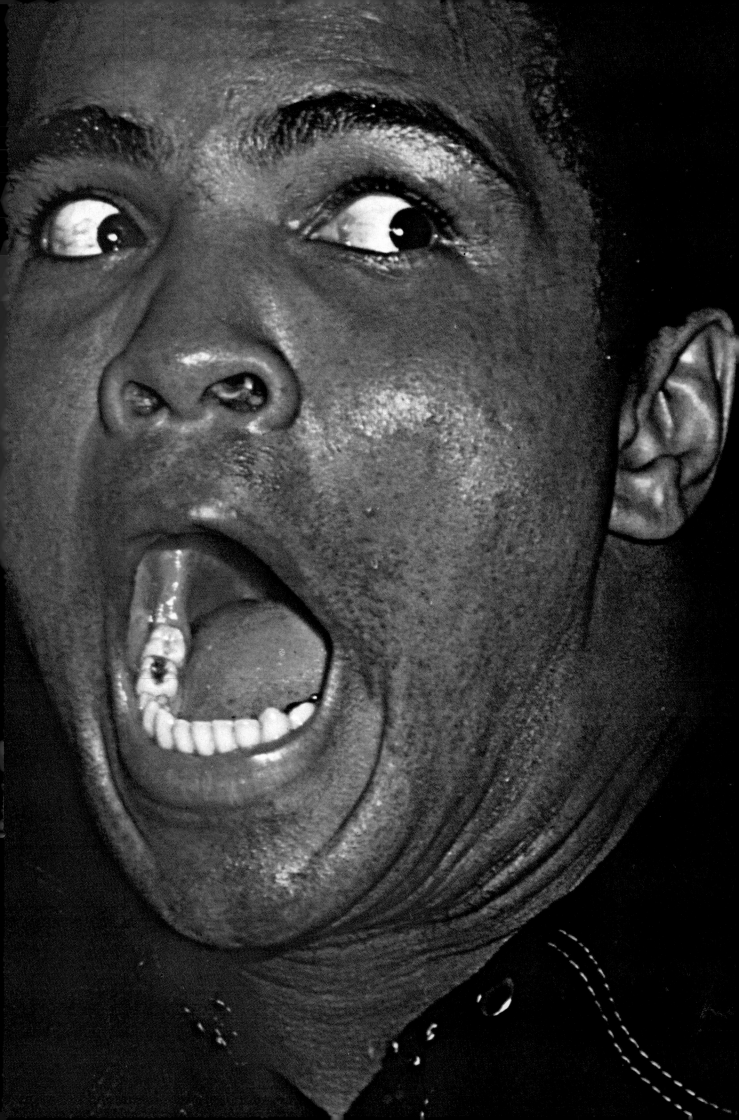

Fight list

Muhammad Ali was born on 17 January 1942. He fought 106 amateur bouts between 1954 and 1960, winning 98 of them. He turned professional in 1960 after winning the Olympic Gold Medal in the light heavyweight division. Here is his pro fight list

Opponent/Place/Date/Decision

Tunney Hunsaker/Louisville, Ky/29.10.60/Won Dec. 6
Herb Siler/Miami Beach, Fla/27.12.60/Won Kayo 4
Tony Esperti/Miami Beach, Fla/17.1.61/Won Kayo 3
Jim Robinson/Miami Beach, Fla/7.2.61/Won Kayo 1
Donnie Fleeman/Miami Beach/21.2.61/Won Kayo 7
Lamar Clark/Louisville, Ky/19.4.61/Won Kayo 2
Duke Sabedong/Las Vegas/26.6.61/Won Dec. 10
Alonzo Johnson/Louisville, Ky/22.7.61/Won Dec. 10
Alex Miteff/Louisville, Ky/7.10.61/Won Kayo 6
Willi Besmanoff/Louisville, Ky/29.11.61/Won Kayo 7
Sonny Banks/New York, N.Y./10.2.62/Won Kayo 4
Don Warner/Miami Beach, Fla/28.2.62/Won Kayo 4
George Logan/Los Angeles, Calif./23.4.62/Won Kayo 4
Billy Daniels/New York, N.Y./19.5.62/Won Kayo 7
Alejandro Lavorante/Los Angeles, Calif./20.7.62/Won Kayo 5
Archie Moore/Los Angeles, Calif./15.11.62/Won Kayo 4
Charlie Powell/Pittsburgh, Pa/24.1.63/Won Kayo 3
Doug Jones/New York, N.Y./13.3.63/Won Dec. 10
Henry Cooper/London, England/18.6.63/Won Kayo 5
Sonny Liston/Miami Beach, Fla/25.2.64/Won Kayo 7
(Won World Heavyweight Championship)
Sonny Liston/Lewiston, Maine/25.5.65/Won Kayo 1
Floyd Patterson/Las Vegas, Nev./22.11.65/Won Kayo 12
George Chuvalo/Toronto, Canada/29.3.66/Won Dec. 15
Henry Cooper/London, England/21.5.66/Won Kayo 6
Brian London/London, England/6.8.66/Won Kayo 3
Karl Mildenberger/Frankfurt, Germany/10.9.66/Won Kayo 12
Cleveland Williams/Houston, Tex./14.11.66/Won Kayo 3
Ernie Terrell/Houston, Tex./6.2.67/Won Dec. 15
Zora Folley/New York, N.Y./22.3.67/Won Kayo 7
Jerry Quarry/Atlanta, Ga/26.10.70/Won Kayo 3
Oscar Bonavena/New York, N.Y./7.12.70/Won Kayo 15
Joe Frazier/New York, N.Y./8.3.71/Lost Dec. 15
(For Undisputed World Heavyweight Title)
Jimmy Ellis/Houston, Tex./26.7.71/Won Kayo 12
Buster Mathis/Houston, Tex./17.11.71/Won Dec. 10
Jurgen Blin/Zurich, Switzerland/26.12.71/Won Kayo 7
Mac Foster/Tokyo, Japan/1.4.72/Won Dec. 15
George Chuvalo/Vancouver, B.C./1.5.71/Won Dec. 12
Jerry Quarry/Las Vegas, Nev./27.6.72/Won Kayo 7
Al 'Blue' Lewis/Dublin, Eire/19.7.72/Won Kayo 11
Floyd Patterson/New York, N.Y./20.9.72/Won Kayo 7
Bob Foster/Stateline, Nev./21.11.72/Won Kayo 8
Joe Bugner/Las Vegas, Nev./14.2.73/Won Dec. 12
Ken Norton/San Diego, Calif./31.3.73/Lost Dec. 12
Ken Norton/Los Angeles, Calif./10.9.73/Won Dec. 12
Rudi Lubbers/Jakarta, Indonesia/20.10.73/Won Dec. 12
Joe Frazier/New York, N.Y./28.1.74/Won Dec. 12
George Foreman/Kinshasa, Zaire/30.10.74/Won Kayo 8
(Regained World Heavyweight Championship)

Acknowledgements The author expresses his thanks to Magnus Linklater the Editor of the *Sunday Times Magazine* in which some of this material first appeared, Judy Groves for editorial research, Guglielmo Galvin of the Rainbow Color Company for excellent photographic colour printing, and Red Saunders and Jacky Garstin for technical photographic help.
The author also expresses his thanks to the following for permission to reproduce photographs: Associated Press; *Boxing News,* Byblos Productions Ltd; Camera 5; Central Press Photos Ltd; *Boxing Illustrated*; Champion Sports Publications, Courier-Journal and Louisville Times; Culver Pictures Inc.; Carl Fischer; Press Association; Popperfoto; *Ring Magazine*; Sport and General Press Agency; UPI, New York